# Prices and Welfare

Abdelkrim Araar • Paolo Verme

# Prices and Welfare

An Introduction to the Measurement of Well-being
when Prices Change

palgrave
macmillan

Abdelkrim Araar
Pavillon J. A. De Sève, Office 2190
Laval University
Quebec
QC, Canada

Paolo Verme
The World Bank
Washington
DC, USA

ISBN 978-3-030-17422-4     ISBN 978-3-030-17423-1   (eBook)
https://doi.org/10.1007/978-3-030-17423-1

This Palgrave Pivot imprint is published by the registered company Springer Nature Switzerland AG.
The registered company address is: Gewerbestrasse 11, 6330 Cham, Switzerland

# FOREWORD

One of the most fundamental roles of economics is to provide policy makers with accurate information on the impact of economic policies, either by modeling ex-ante the effects of potential policies or by evaluating ex-post the effects of policies that have been implemented. Among the effects to be considered, those of price changes are among the most relevant for household well-being. Whether price changes appear in the financial market (interest rates), the labor market (wages), the consumer market (commodity prices) or the government sector (taxes and subsidies), they can have important consequences both for household income and for the distribution of such incomes. Yet, the impact of price changes on household well-being is one of the most sensitive topics in economic research and possibly one of the major sources of contention in empirical economics.

This book provides the foundations for understanding and measuring the impact of price changes on household well-being in a unifying format that is rarely seen in economic textbooks. It first provides a simple and intuitive graphical representation of the problem, clarifying in the process the normative foundations behind the different types of measures of well-being adopted by the economic profession. It then provides a rigorous mathematical illustration of those measures as well as possible computation methods. Next, it provides illustrations on how these measurement and computational methods can be used in empirical applications under different scenarios and also offers a simple toolkit designed to help practitioners that need to make choices between those methods. Finally, it provides statistical instruments to increase the accuracy of estimation procedures and offers necessary coding in Stata to estimate the measurement and computational methods reviewed.

The authors are both experts in the field and former colleagues of mine. During my time as Economics Professor at Université Laval, I had the pleasure of working with Abdelkrim Araar and Paolo Verme in the context of different projects. They are both accomplished economists with extensive experience in the measurement of poverty and income distribution, and they bring together a combination of skills ranging from theory to programming, and from empirics to policy making, that is unique and suits the scope of this book particularly well. In my view, this is one of the most useful treatises on the subject of prices and household well-being and one that can be recommended to undergraduate and graduate students, empirical economists and practitioners in economic policy.

Minister of Families, Children and Social              Jean-Yves Duclos
Development, Government of Canada
Quebec, QC, Canada

# ACKNOWLEDGMENTS

This book is the byproduct of a five-year period spent by the authors working on subsidy reforms in the North Africa and Middle East (MENA) region. As the Arab Spring unfolded starting from 2011 and oil prices increased, many of the countries in the region found themselves with large budget deficits caused by energy and food subsidies inherited from the old regimes. Confronted with these new challenges, these countries requested support from the World Bank to reduce subsidies while managing complex political reforms. The authors of this book would spend the next five years working with governments in the region to reform subsidies. In the process, they developed a subsidy simulation model (www.subsim.org) and published a book recording the results of these simulations across the region (*The Quest for Subsidy Reforms in the Middle East and North Africa Region*, Springer, 2017). The book we present here complements this work by providing the theory, algorithms and coding that was used for the model and the book on the MENA region. It also expands this work by adapting the theory and empirics to suit any kind of price reform and assist practitioners and policy makers in taking informed decisions. The book is dedicated to our parents.

Quebec, QC, Canada                                            Abdelkrim Araar
Washington, DC, USA                                             Paolo Verme

# ABSTRACT

What is the welfare effect of a price change? This simple question is one of the most relevant and controversial questions in microeconomic theory and one of the main sources of errors in empirical economics. This book returns to this question with the objective of providing a general framework for the use of theoretical contributions in empirical works. Welfare measures and computational methods are compared to test how these choices result in different welfare measurement under different scenarios of price changes. As a rule of thumb and irrespective of parameter choices, welfare measures converge to approximately the same result for price changes below 10 percent. Above this threshold, these measures start to diverge significantly. Budget shares play an important role in explaining such divergence. Single or multiple price changes influence results visibly, whereas the choice of demand system has a surprisingly minor role. Under standard utility assumptions, the Laspeyres and Paasche variations are always the outer bounds of welfare estimates, and the consumer's surplus is the median estimate. The book also introduces a new simple welfare approximation, clarifies the relation between Taylor's approximations and the income and substitution effects and provides an example for treating non-linear pricing.

# CONTENTS

1   Introduction                                                             1
    *References*                                                             6

2   Assumptions and Measures                                                 9
    *2.1   Assumptions*                                                      9
    *2.2   Measures*                                                        11
          *2.2.1   Definitions*                                            11
          *2.2.2   Geometric Interpretation*                               14
    *References*                                                           17

3   Theory and Computation                                                  19
    *3.1   Computation*                                                     19
          *3.1.1   Index Numbers*                                          20
          *3.1.2   Demand Functions*                                       20
          *3.1.3   Elasticity*                                             23
          *3.1.4   Taylor's Approximations*                                25
          *3.1.5   Vartia's Approximation*                                 38
          *3.1.6   Breslaw and Smith's Approximation*                      40
          *3.1.7   The Ordinary Differential Equations Methods*            40
          *3.1.8   Relational Approach*                                    42
    *References*                                                           44

**4    Empirical Applications**                                        47
   *4.1    Applications*                                  47
      *4.1.1    Individual Welfare*                   48
      *4.1.2    Social Welfare*                       61
   *References*                                         73

**5    Conclusion**                                                    75

**Appendices**                                                        79
   *A.1    Demand Systems*                                79
      *A.1.1    Linear Demand (LD)*                   79
      *A.1.2    Log Linear Demand (LLD)*              79
      *A.1.3    The Linear Expenditure System (LES)*   80
      *A.1.4    The Almost Ideal Demand System (AIDS)*   82
      *A.1.5    The Quadratic Almost Ideal Demand System*
          *(QUAIDS)*                            84
      *A.1.6    Exact Affine Stone Index (EASI)*      85
   *B.1    Nonlinear Price Changes and Well-Being*        87
   *C.1    Stata Codes*                                   90
   *References*                                         96

**Index**                                                             97

# MATHEMATICAL NOTATIONS

**Welfare Measures**

| | |
|---|---|
| $CV$ | Compensating variation |
| $EV$ | Equivalent variation |
| $CS$ | Consumer's surplus variation |
| $LV$ | Laspeyres variation |
| $PV$ | Paasche variation |
| $S$ | Substitution effect |
| $I$ | Income effect |

**Functions**

| | |
|---|---|
| $u(.)$ | Direct utility |
| $v(.)$ | Indirect utility |
| $e(.)$ | Expenditure |
| $D_k(p)$ | Demand |
| $x_k(P, m)$ | Marshallian demand |
| $h_k(P, m)$ | Hicksian demand |
| $\Delta(.)$ | Absolute variation |
| $d(.)$ | Proportional variation |
| $\lambda(.)$ | Proportion of the error term |

**Vectors**

| | |
|---|---|
| $p$ | Price |
| $x$ | Quantity |
| $m$ | Income |
| $e$ | Expenditure |
| $s_k$ | Expenditure share of good $k$ |

**Scalars**

| | |
|---|---|
| $\vartheta$ | Income elasticity |
| $\eta$ | Non-compensated price elasticity |

**Indexes**

| | |
|---|---|
| $k = 1, 2, \ldots, n$ | Products (subscript) |
| $t = a, b$ | State/time (superscript) |
| $o = 1, 2, \ldots, n$ | Taylor degree of approximation (superscript) |

# LIST OF FIGURES

Fig. 2.1    Welfare measures                                                            15
Fig. 3.1    Price and welfare changes                                                   35
Fig. 3.2    Taylor approximation and the substitution effect                           35
Fig. 3.3    The Vartia algorithm to compute the $CV$ measurement                        39
Fig. 4.1    Well-being and price changes                                                49
Fig. 4.2    Error size and price change                                                 49
Fig. 4.3    Price and welfare changes and the substitution effect                      51
Fig. 4.4    Price and welfare changes (multiple price changes)                         52
Fig. 4.5    Price, expenditure share and welfare changes                               53
Fig. 4.6    Restricted information and welfare measurement                             54
Fig. 4.7    Cobb–Douglas vs. elasticity and Taylor methods                             55
Fig. 4.8    Cobb–Douglas vs. elasticity and Taylor methods (error size)               56
Fig. 4.9    Taylor approximation and welfare change                                     57
Fig. 4.10   Contour map of the GAP estimations by price changes and
            expenditure shares                                                         62
Fig. 4.11   The difference between welfare measurements                                66
Fig. 4.12   The welfare measurements and the sampling errors                           67
Fig. 4.13   First-order pro-poor price reform curve (small price changes)             71
Fig. 4.14   Second-order pro-poor price reform curve (small price
            changes)                                                                   71
Fig. 4.15   First-order pro-poor price reform curve (large price changes)             72
Fig. 4.16   Second-order pro-poor price reform curve (large price
            changes)                                                                   73

# List of Tables

| | | |
|---|---|---|
| Table 3.1 | Cobb–Douglas and the Taylor approximation | 37 |
| Table 3.2 | CV and EV estimations with Vartia's algorithm | 40 |
| Table 3.3 | Euler and RK4 method simulations | 43 |
| Table 4.1 | Summary of welfare measure, computation methods and functional requirements | 58 |
| Table 4.2 | Welfare impact simulations with different measures, computation methods and scenarios | 59 |
| Table 4.3 | The normalized GAP estimations by price changes and expenditure shares | 63 |
| Table 4.4 | Estimated statistics for the fourth quintile | 69 |
| Table B.1 | The price schedule | 88 |
| Table B.2 | Nonlinear price schedule: an illustrative example | 88 |

CHAPTER 1

# Introduction

In economics, there are two established traditions for the measurement of individual utility, well-being or welfare.[1] The first tradition pioneered by Edgeworth (1881) argues that utility can be measured directly with a "hedonimeter" capable of capturing the physiological phenomenon of happiness. This tradition enjoyed very few followers until the emergence and establishment of happiness economics and prospect theory, two relatively new strands of the economics literature that attempt, in different ways, to directly measure utility. The happiness literature tends to measure happiness with subjective questions on happiness and life satisfaction. The prospect theory literature has measured utility, for example, with the measurement of physiological pain.

The second tradition pioneered by Fisher (1892) argues that utility cannot be measured directly in any sensible way and that it is necessary to derive utility indirectly from the observation of behavioral choices.[2] If we assimilate Paul Samuelson's theory of revealed preferences with this tradition, we can then argue that this has been the prevalent welfare theory taught in economics over the past century. Interestingly, while Bentham himself equated happiness with utility (as in the happiness literature),

---

[1] This book uses these three terms as synonyms and will use them interchangeably as needed.

[2] See Colander (2007), for a historical comparative analysis of these two traditions.

© The Author(s) 2019
A. Araar, P. Verme, *Prices and Welfare*,
https://doi.org/10.1007/978-3-030-17423-1_1

1

he also thought that utility was embedded in objects (as in the revealed preferences literature):

> By utility is meant that property in any object, whereby it tends to produce benefit, advantage, pleasure, good, or happiness, (all this in the present case comes to the same thing) or (what comes again to the same thing) to prevent the happening of mischief, pain, evil, or unhappiness to the party whose interest is considered (p. 2, Bentham ([1789]1907)).

This book focuses on changes in welfare derived from changes in prices following the second tradition of indirect welfare measurement. The main purpose is to estimate the difference in welfare that derives from the choice of different welfare measures and clarify the key factors that determine such differences. We consider five measures (henceforth called "welfare measures") that have been proposed by the microeconomics literature to measure welfare changes since the seminal paper by Hicks (1942): (1) consumer's surplus variation ($CS$ for short), (2) compensating variation ($CV$), (3) equivalent variation ($EV$), (4) Laspeyres variation ($LV$) and (5) Paasche variation ($PV$).

Building on previous contributions, we aim to (1) review the essential microeconomics literature; (2) organize and simplify this literature in a way that can be easily understood by researchers and practitioners with different backgrounds providing algebraic, geometric, computational and empirical illustrations; (3) identify and measure the essential differences across methods and test how these differences affect empirical results; (4) provide guidelines for the use of alternative approaches under imperfect information on utility, demand systems, elasticities and more generally incomes and quantities; and (5) provide computational codes in Stata for the application of all welfare measures and computational methods.

While the theoretical literature regularly offers excellent review papers on the topic (see, e.g. Harberger (1971); King (1983); Slesnick (1998) and Fleurbaey (2009)), we believe that this literature remains short of providing simple guidelines for practitioners. On the other hand, the empirical literature, which is very rich and varied, remains short of explaining clearly the microeconomic foundations that justify the choice of one welfare measure over another. Our main goal is to bridge these two traditions and fill these gaps in an effort to serve practitioners working with micro data, particularly those focusing on poor countries and poor people. Presumably, measuring the impact on welfare due to price changes is of interest to the policy maker for social and distributive policies. The impact of price changes on the rich is typically small in relative terms and less of a concern than the impact on the middle class or the poor. Hence, our focus on the poor.

We will follow what is sometimes called the "marginal approach". This is the estimation of direct effect of a price change on welfare keeping the nominal budget constraint or income constant. Price changes can eventually affect incomes of producers and other agents, and these effects can be important (see, e.g. Ravallion (1990) and Jacoby (2015)). However, this complicates substantially our analysis, and we opted to exclude income, supply, partial or general equilibrium effects from the book. We will therefore follow the more common tradition of the marginal approach as in Ahmad and Stern (1984, 1991), Creedy (1998, 2001), Deaton (1989), Minot and Dewina (2013) and Ferreira et al. (2011). See also Creedy and van de Ven (1997) on the impact of marginal changes in food subsidies on Foster, Greer and Thorbecke (FGT) poverty indexes.

The book will cover a range of computation methods (henceforth called "welfare computations") that have been proposed by the literature over the years including methods based on different demand systems, Taylor approximations, the Vartia method, the Breslaw and Smith method, ordinary differential equations methods and a simple method based on knowledge of elasticity. There are of course many more methods proposed by the literature and evidence on how these methods perform. Hausman and Newey (1995), for example, derive estimates of demand curves and the consumer surplus applying non-parametric regression models. Banks et al. (1996) derive second-order approximations of welfare effects and show how first-order approximations can produce large biases by ignoring the distribution of substitution effects. In this book, we restrict the analysis to the most popular methods cited above.

With respect to computation methods, our contribution is to clarify the relation between the five measures initially introduced by Hicks and their computation methods. Some authors may argue that some of the computation methods we discuss such as Taylor's approximations of a certain degree are welfare measures themselves and different from the five measures listed above. In this work, we will clarify the distinction between core measures and computation methods. In addition, we clarify the decomposition of higher-order Taylor's approximations in substitution and income effects and propose a simple computation method based on known elasticities.

The book does not focus on the analysis or construction of demand systems. This literature is rather vast and offers several alternatives. One of the critiques to simple linear expenditure systems was that they fail to consider the Engel law, the variation of the income-expenditure relation across the income distribution. Muellbauer (1976), Deaton and Muellbauer (1980a,b) and Jorgenson et al. (1982) contributions helped to place the Working-Leser Engel curve specification within integrable consumer theory, thereby starting to address this issue. Recent empirical work has shown that the popular AID system does not take into consideration the full curvature of the Engel curve. Banks et al. (1997) showed that Working-Leser Engel types of curves may be insufficient to describe consumption behavior across income groups. They derive a demand model based on an integrable quadratic logarithmic expenditure share system and show that this model fits UK data better than the Working-Leser Engel types of models, particularly for selected commodities. Blundell et al. (2007) later showed that behavior changes across different types of goods with some goods approaching a linear or quadratic shape while others having different forms. More recently, Lewbel and Pendakur (2009) proposed the Exact Affine Stone Index (EASI) implicit Marshallian demand system. In the words of the authors:

> In contrast to the AID system, the EASI demand system also allows for flexible interactions between prices and expenditures, permits almost any functional form for Engel curves, and allows error terms in the model to correspond to unobserved preference heterogeneity random utility parameters (p. 29).

Recent empirical works that attempted to estimate demand systems directly from data in developing countries include Attanasio et al. (2013) and Osei-Asare and Eghan (2013).

With respect to demand systems, our contribution is to compare the behavior of different welfare measures using alternative demand systems including simple Cobb-Douglas (CD), Linear Expenditure System (LES), the Almost Ideal Demand System (AIDS), the Quadratic Almost Ideal Demand System (QUAIDS) and the Exact Affine Stone Index (EASI). The book finds that the difference in welfare measurement is minimal as compared to changes in other parameters such as the price change or the budget share.

Results of this book can be relevant for a wide set of issues empirical economists are confronted with. Changes in prices occur for a variety of reasons. They may be induced by global shocks as it was the case for the global rise in commodity prices during the first decade of the 2000s or the 2008 global financial crisis, or they may be due to domestic shocks such as those induced by variations in local climatic conditions. Price changes may also occur as a result of economic policies such as changes in taxes, wages, subsidies or social transfers. In all these cases, the policy maker may want to estimate the impact on well-being *ex-post* (e.g. in the case of economic shocks) or *ex-ante* (e.g. in the case of economic policies). The work proposed applies to both cases and provides guidelines for macro- or micro-economists or for macro- or micro-simulation exercises of economic shocks or policy reforms.

Measuring changes in welfare due to changes in prices is also an issue very relevant for adjusting welfare measures (such as the poverty headcount) spatially or longitudinally and therefore measuring changes in poverty over time correctly. As the latest round of the global Purchasing Parity Power (PPP) surveys has shown, changes in data on prices can change welfare measurements very significantly. Changing measure or method for estimating welfare effects of price changes can obviously amplify or reduce the effect of price changes. Practitioners as well as international organizations engaged in measuring the impact of price changes on welfare give surprisingly little weight to the choice of estimation method. For example, the World Bank and the IMF use as methods of choice for spatial and longitudinal price adjustments the Laspeyres or Paasche indexes, while they almost invariably use the Laspeyres index when simulating the impact of price changes on welfare, and this is often irrespective of the magnitude of the price change. Theoretical economists, on the other hand, tend to privilege the equivalent variation or consumer's surplus measures when it comes to measure changes in welfare due to price changes. A priori, these are normative decisions and good arguments can be found to justify each of these choices. But the outcomes of these choices can be very different in terms of welfare measurement, and this should be very clear to anyone making these choices.

The book is organized as follows. The next chapter provides the underlying assumptions of the models used. In addition, it presents the definitions of the welfare measures used and provides a simple geometrical interpretation. Chapter 3 reviews the computational approaches provided by the literature under specific assumptions or degree of information.

Chapter 4 tests how the measures and computations proposed diverge as prices and other key parameters vary. This chapter also discusses statistical inference and stochastic dominance when individual welfare measures are aggregated at the societal level. Finally, Chapter 5 concludes summarizing results and providing basic recommendations for practitioners.

## REFERENCES

AHMAD, E. AND N. STERN (1984): "The Theory of Reform and Indian Indirect Taxes," *Journal of Public Economics*, 25, 259–98.

AHMAD, E. AND N. H. STERN (1991): *The Theory and Practice of Tax Reform in Developing Countries*, Cambridge.

ATTANASIO, O., V. DI MARO, V. LECHENE, AND D. PHILLIPS (2013): "Welfare consequences of food prices increases: Evidence from rural Mexico," *Journal of Development Economics*, 104, 136–151.

BANKS, J., R. BLUNDELL, AND A. LEWBEL (1996): "Tax Reform and Welfare Measurement: Do We Need Demand System Estimation?" *Economic Journal*, 106, 1227–41.

—— (1997): "Quadratic Engel Curves And Consumer Demand," *The Review of Economics and Statistics*, 79, 527–539.

BENTHAM, J. ([1789]1907): *An Introduction to the Principles of Morals and Legislation*.

BLUNDELL, R., C. XIAOHONG, AND D. KRISTENSEN (2007): "Semi-Nonparametric IV Estimation of Shape-Invariant Engel Curves," *Econometrica*, 75(6), 1613–1669. Econometric Society.

COLANDER, D. (2007): "Retrospectives: Edgeworth's Hedonimeter and the Quest to Measure Utility," *Journal of Economic Perspectives*, 21, 215–226.

CREEDY, J. (1998): "Measuring the Welfare Effects of Price Changes: A Convenient Parametric Approach," *Australian Economic Papers*, 37, 137–51.

—— (2001): "Indirect Tax Reform and the Role of Exemptions," *Fiscal Studies*, 22, 457–86.

CREEDY, J. AND J. VAN DE VEN (1997): "The Distributional Effects of Inflation in Australia 1980–1995," *Australian Economic Review*, 30, 125–43.

DEATON, A. (1989): "Rice Prices and Income Distribution in Thailand: A Nonparametric Analysis," *Economic Journal*, 99, 1–37.

DEATON, A. AND J. MUELLBAUER (1980a): "An Almost Ideal Demand System," *American Economic Review*, 70, 312–336.

—— (1980b): *Economics and Consumer Behavior*, Cambridge: Cambridge University Press.

EDGEWORTH, F. (1881): *Mathematical Psychics: An Essay on the Application of Mathematics to the Moral Sciences*, vol. 10, C.K. Paul and co.

FERREIRA, F. H. G., A. FRUTTERO, P. LEITE, AND L. LUCCHETTI (2011): "Rising food prices and household welfare : evidence from Brazil in 2008," Policy Research Working Paper Series 5652, The World Bank.

FISHER, I. (1892): "Mathematical Investigations in the Theory of Value and Prices," *Transactions of the Connecticut Academy of Sciences and Arts*, 9, 1–124.

FLEURBAEY, M. (2009): "Beyond GDP: The Quest for a Measure of Social Welfare," *Journal of Economic Literature*, 47, 1029–75.

HARBERGER, A. C. (1971): "Three Basic Postulates for Applied Welfare Economics: An Interpretive Essay," *Journal of Economic Literature*, 9, 785–97.

HAUSMAN, J. AND W. NEWEY (1995): "Nonparametric Estimation of Exact Consumers Surplus and Deadweight Loss," *Econometrica*, 63(6), 1445–1476.

HICKS, J. R. (1942): "Consumers Surplus and Index-Numbers," *The Review of Economic Studies*, 9, 126–137.

JACOBY, H. G. (2015): "Food prices, Wages, and Welfare in Rural India," *Economic Inquiry*, 54, 159–176.

JORGENSON, D. W., L. J. LAU, AND T. M. STOKER (1982): "The Transcendental Logarithmic Model of Aggregate Consumer Behavior," in R. BASMANN and G. RHODES (eds.), Advances in Econometrics, vol. 1 (Greenwich, Ct: JAI Press, 1982).

KING, M. (1983): "Welfare Analysis of Tax Reforms Using Household Data," *Journal of Public Economics*, 21, 183–214.

LEWBEL, A. AND K. PENDAKUR (2009): "Tricks with Hicks: The EASI Demand System," *American Economic Review*, 99, 827–63.

MINOT, N. AND R. DEWINA (2013): "Impact of food price changes on household welfare in Ghana:," Tech. rep.

MUELLBAUER, J. (1976): "Community Preferences and the Representative Consumer," *Econometrica*, 44(5), 979–999. Econometric Society.

OSEI-ASARE, Y. B. AND M. EGHAN (2013): "Food Price Inflation And Consumer Welfare In Ghana," *International Journal of Food and Agricultural Economics (IJFAEC)*, 1.

RAVALLION, M. (1990): "Rural Welfare Effects of Food Price Changes under Induced Wage Responses: Theory and Evidence for Bangladesh," *Oxford Economic Papers*, 42, 574–85.

SLESNICK, D. T. (1998): "Empirical Approaches to the Measurement of Welfare," *Journal of Economic Literature*, 36, 2108–2165.

# CHAPTER 2

# Assumptions and Measures

## 2.1 ASSUMPTIONS

To restrict the boundaries of the discussion that follows, we will make a number of standard assumptions. Consumers have a preference ordering $R$ defined in the commodity space $X$ and have well-behaved utility functions (monotonic and strictly convex preferences) and single-valued, continuously differentiable demand function where prices are strictly positive. The basic axioms of consumer theory are observed (consumer preferences are complete, reflexive and transitive). Preferences are homothetic so that $(x_1, x_2) \prec (y_1, y_2) \Leftrightarrow (tx_1, tx_2) \prec (ty_1, ty_2)$ for any $t > 0$. Most of the derived results will concern all of the consumer functional forms that obey the basic consumer axioms.[1]

The demand function is generated by $R$ and is not necessarily observable with data. Consumers maximize utility and operate on the budget constraint with marginal utility of income being constant throughout the space concerned by price changes. The commodity $X$ space includes two normal goods where the first good $x_1$ is subject to price changes and the second good $x_2$ represents the bundle of all other goods available to the consumer, which may or may not be subject to price change.

---

[1] Recall that homothetic functions make the money-metric utility functions concave, which is a desirable property for welfare analyses (Ali Khan and Schlee 2017).

© The Author(s) 2019
A. Araar, P. Verme, *Prices and Welfare*,
https://doi.org/10.1007/978-3-030-17423-1_2

We also assume that the budget constraint remains nominally fixed under price changes so that any price increase (reduction) results in a loss (gain) in real incomes. These assumptions imply short-term decisions, no savings and no inter-temporal choices. Other than being standard neoclassical assumptions, we justify these choices on the ground that we are particularly concerned with the poor and developing countries where, by definition, savings are close to zero and consumers spend all their budget on current consumption.

Individual and household preferences are considered as one and the same. We also consider identical behavior and utility functions across consumers and no utility inter-dependence. Social welfare is the non-weighted sum of the outcomes of individual (household) choices implying that we ignore any impact on the non-household sector. As discussed in the introduction, we consider indirect utility functions on the assumption that utility cannot be observed directly and we use money-metric utility functions as proposed by McKenzie (1957). The underlying idea is that an indirect utility function can be represented in terms of an expenditure function.

The essential problem we are trying to solve is how to measure welfare changes when the price of at least one of the goods considered changes and if utility, demand or both are not known. We consider a consumer who chooses a bundle of two goods $x = \{x_1, x_2\}$ subject to prices $p = \{p_1, p_2\}$. The consumer maximizes a well-behaved utility function $u(x)$ under a budget constraint $m = p_1 x_1 + p_2 x_2$ and a demand system $D = d(p, m)$ and is subject to a price shock ($\Delta p_1$). What is known are current prices $(p_1, p_2)$, current quantities $x_1, x_2$, current budget $(m)$ and the price change $\Delta p_1$. What is not necessarily known are utility $u(x)$ and demand functions $d(p, m)$ and therefore the change in quantities $\Delta x_1$ and $\Delta x_2$ and the change in utility $\Delta u$ due to the price change $\Delta p_1$. The central question is how to estimate the change in welfare $\Delta u$ in money terms and under different degrees of information on the other parameters.

Note that we will talk of *partial effects* when we consider variations in prices of only one product and *general effects* when we consider simultaneous variations in prices of more than one product. We will mostly refer to the Marshallian demand function in place of Walrasian or uncompensated demand functions and to the Hicksian demand function in place of compensated demand function.

In real life, researchers are confronted with a general scarcity of information on consumers' behavior, and this is more so in developing and poor countries where data are scarce. In what follows, we will review the different ways of approximating changes in welfare under different degrees of information on consumers' behavior.

## 2.2    MEASURES

### 2.2.1    Definitions

We consider five popular measures of welfare change under price variations which were already outlined by Hicks over 70 years ago[2]: *consumer's surplus variation* (CS), *equivalent variation* (EV), *compensating variation* (CV), *Laspeyres variation* (LV) and *Paasche variation* (PV). In this first section, we simply outline the concepts and the basic formulations of these measures.

The **consumer's surplus variation (CS)**[3] was initially introduced by Marshall and defined as *"The excess of the price which he would be willing to pay rather than go without the thing, over that which he actually does pay, is the economic measure of this surplus satisfaction. It may be called consumer's surplus."* (Marshall (1890) 1961). By definition, this measurement requires knowledge of the Marshallian demand function (the "willingness to pay" function) and can be represented by the area under this curve delimited by two prices. One possible formulation of the $CS$ is therefore as follows[4]:

$$CS = \int_{p^a}^{p^b} D(p)dp \qquad (2.1)$$

where $p^a$ and $p^b$ represent initial and final prices, respectively, and $D(p)$ is a generic demand function that applies equally to all consumers.

Perhaps the main supporter of this concept as a measure of welfare change has been Harberger (1971) with his letter to the profession published in the *Journal of Economic Literature*. As described in this paper, the five main criticisms to the $CS$ approach state that this approach (1) is valid only when the marginal utility of real incomes is constant, (2) does not take into account distributional changes derived from price changes, (3) is

[2] See Hicks (1942).
[3] Note the use of $CS$ for consumer's surplus variation rather than consumer surplus.
[4] See Layard and Walters (1978).

a partial equilibrium approach, (4) does not apply to large price changes and (5) is made obsolete by the revealed preferences approach.

By analogy with national accounts, Harberger (1971) responded to each of the five criticisms, but on point (1) further research has shown that the conditions for the CV approach to apply are more restrictive than initially thought. As shown by Chipman and Moore (1977), changes in consumer's surplus are single-valued and ordinarily equivalent to changes in utility under the conditions of utility maximization, homogeneous utility, integrable demand functions and constant marginal utility. In addition, with changes in prices that affect more than one product, the $CS$ approach is "path dependent", meaning that the estimation of the welfare change will be different depending on which price changes first. These two critiques have induced scholars to revalue other methods and approximations of welfare change (see Slesnick (1998) for a full critique of the $CS$ method).

The **compensating variation (CV)** was first named by Hicks in his "Value and Capital", but it was Henderson (1941) who first clarified the distinction between $CS$ and $CV$. Hicks (1942) later accepted this distinction and also introduced the concept of **equivalent variation (EV)** to distinguish Henderson's concept of $CV$ when welfare change is evaluated at final rather than initial prices. The $CV$ is the monetary compensation required to bring the consumer back to the original utility level after the price change. The $EV$ is the monetary change required to obtain the same level of utility after the price change. For changes from $p^a$ to $p^b$ of one product, these two variations can be represented as[5]:

$$CV = e(p^a, v^a) - e(p^b, v^a) \qquad (2.2)$$

$$= \int_{p^a}^{p^b} h(p, v^a).dp \qquad (2.3)$$

$$EV = e(p^a, v^b) - e(p^b, v^b) \qquad (2.4)$$

$$= \int_{p^a}^{p^b} h(p, v^b).dp \qquad (2.5)$$

[5] See Layard and Walters (1978) or Dixit and Weller (1979).

where $v$ and $e$ represent generic indirect utility and expenditure functions.[6]

The **Laspeyres variation (LV)** is defined as the exact change in income necessary to purchase, after the price variation, the same bundle of goods purchased before the price variation. The **Paasche variation (PV)** is defined as the exact change in income required to purchase the final bundle of goods at initial prices. Hence, possible representations of the two indexes are the following:

$$LV = e(p^b, x^a) - e(p^a, x^a) \qquad (2.6)$$

$$PV = e(p^b, x^b) - e(p^a, x^b) \qquad (2.7)$$

The $LV$ and the $PV$ derive from index number theory initially proposed by Fisher (1922). As discussed by Fleurbaey (2009), index number theory has developed in three directions. The first direction aims at defining desirable properties of an index and finds indexes that satisfy these properties. For example, Diewert (1992) shows that the original indexes proposed by Fisher satisfy a set of 21 desirable axioms which make these indexes superior to others. The second direction is a tradition that seeks indexes that depend only on prices and quantities and that are good approximations of welfare changes. Diewert (1992) has shown, for example, that it is possible to find functional forms of the expenditure function that are both simple and flexible and that result in indexes such as the geometric mean of the Laspeyres and Paasche indexes. The third direction initiated by Samuelson and Swamy (1974) seeks indexes that depend on individual preferences such as the money-metric utility function. In this chapter, we will not discuss further these different developments of index number theory. What is important to stress here is that the $LV$ and $PV$ indexes are routinely used to measure welfare changes under price changes and to adjust longitudinally and spatially welfare measures such as the poverty headcount index.

As already clear from these first formulations, while the $CS$, $CV$ and $EV$ methods require knowledge of utility functions and demand functions, the $LV$ and $PV$ as defined above require information on the demand function only. The difference between measures becomes clearer when we

---

[6] Recall that the optimal indirect utility provides the consumer's maximal attainable utility given a price vector and a given amount of income. Conversely, optimal expenditure provides the minimum amount of money an individual needs to spend to achieve some level of utility.

illustrate these methods geometrically in the next section whereas we will see that it is possible to estimate these measures also in the absence of direct knowledge of the Marshallian demand function. This is particularly important for countries where it is not possible to measure this demand function directly because of data constraints.

### 2.2.2   Geometric Interpretation

Figure 2.1 illustrates the five estimation methods discussed in a classic geometric setting. In the top panel, the initial budget line is the continuous blue line and the initial equilibrium is at $A$. The slope of this curve is $-p^a$. After an increase in price from $p^a$ to $p^b$, the budget constraint curve rotates as shown by the red line adjusting to a slope $-p^b$ and the final state is reached in $B$.

The $LV$ measurement evaluates the change in welfare with the initial bundle of goods. Thus $LV = -x^a(p^b - p^a)$ which is (minus) the distance between $A$ and $A_2$. Similarly, we can evaluate the potential change in expenditure with the final quantities such that $PV = -x^b(p^b - p^a)$, which is (minus) the distance between $B$ and $B_2$. The $CV$ is the required budget to offset the loss in well-being with the new prices. This amount is equal to $-\overline{BB}_1$, which leads to $D$. The $EV$ is the price equivalent loss in well-being. It equals $-\overline{AA}_1$, which leads to $C$.

The bottom panel of Fig. 2.1 shows the geometric interpretation of the five methods in the case of a price increase from $p^a$ to $p^b$, a change in quantity from $x^a$ to $x^b$, linear demand schedules derived from known utility functions and changes in the price of only one product (assumptions derived from the top panel). Following from the definitions provided in the previous section, the $CS$ is the area below the Marshallian demand curve and between initial and final prices, which is the area delimited by points $p^a E A p^b$. Consequently, the $EV$ is equal to the area $p^a C A p^b$, the $CV$ is equal to the area $p^a E D p^b$, the $LV$ is the rectangle $p^a E F p^b$ which is equal to $-x^a \Delta p$ and the $PV$ is equal to the area of the rectangle $p^a B A p^b$, which is equal to $-x^b \Delta p$.

From Fig. 2.1, which is inspired by Hicks (1942), we can derive a first set of results:

1. For a normal good, $LV < CV < CS < EV < PV$ if $dp \neq 0$ and the demand schedules are not perfectly elastic or inelastic (see also Hicks (1942), Willig (1976) and Cory et al. (1981)).

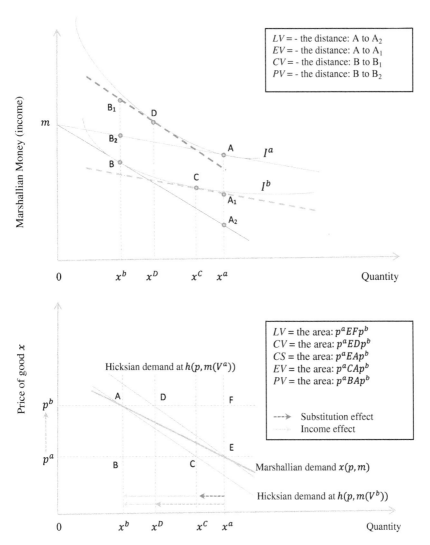

**Fig. 2.1** Welfare measures. Source: Authors' design inspired from Hicks (1942)

2. The welfare effect is bounded between $LV = -x^a dp$ and $PV = -x^b dp$.
3. $LV \neq CV \neq CS \neq EV \neq PV$ if $dp \neq 0$ and the demand schedules are not perfectly elastic or inelastic.
4. The difference between the different measures depends on the size of the price change, on the utility function and on the corresponding demand functions.

We can also express result (1) above in terms of changes in prices and quantities as follows:

$$x^a dp > (x^a + x^c)dp/2 > (x^a + x^b)dp/2 > (x^e + x^b)dp/2 > x^b dp \qquad (2.8)$$

By dividing by $dp$ and multiplying by 2, we obtain the relation between the different methods in terms of quantities only[7]:

$$2x^a > (x^a + x^c) > (x^a + x^b) > (x^e + x^b) > 2x^b \qquad (2.9)$$

From the inequality above, we can then derive the following additional results:

5. With a perfectly inelastic (vertical) Marshallian demand schedule, $x^a = x^b$ and the welfare effect is only determined by prices and estimated at $x^a dp$. It is also evident that $LV = CV = CS = EV = PV$ so that it is irrelevant which approach is used to the measurement of welfare.
6. Vice versa, with a perfectly elastic (horizontal) demand schedule, the consumer is not willing to buy any quantity at the new price ($x^b = 0$) and the welfare effects will be equal to the loss of the original welfare $x^a p^a$. In this case too, the welfare estimates will not depend on the approach followed and $LV = CV = CS = EV = PV$.

In essence, changes in welfare $\Delta V$ will be bounded between $(-)x^a dp$ and $(-)x^b dp$. Within these boundaries, $LV \neq CV \neq CS \neq EV \neq PV$ if $dp \neq 0$ and the different approaches will produce different estimates of

---

[7] Note that this result is based on the assumptions of moderate change in price or in the case of a straightforward line shape of the demand function.

welfare change. The difference in these estimates, in turn, will depend on the size of the price change, on the shape of the utility function and on the derived demand function. Choices concerning these last two parameters led to the use of different computational strategies for the five indicators of welfare change illustrated. These strategies are discussed in the next chapter.

## REFERENCES

ALI KHAN, M. AND E. SCHLEE (2017): "The nonconcavity of money-metric utility: A new formulation and proof," *Economics Letters*, 154, 10–12.

CHIPMAN, J. AND J. MOORE (1977): *The Scope of Consumer's Surplus Arguments*, Reprint series.

CORY, D. C., R. L. GUM, W. E. MARTIN, AND R. F. BROKKEN (1981): "Simplified Measurement of Consumer Welfare Change," *American Journal of Agricultural Economics*, 63, 715–717.

DIEWERT, W. E. (1992): "Fisher Ideal Output, Input, and Productivity Indexes Revisited," *Journal of Productivity Analysis*, 3, 211–4.

DIXIT, A. K. AND P. A. WELLER (1979): "The Three Consumer's Surpluses," *Economica*, 46, 125–35.

FISHER, I. (1922): *The Making of Index Numbers: A Study of Their Varieties, Tests, and Reliability*, Publications of the Pollak Foundation for Economic Research, Houghton Mifflin.

FLEURBAEY, M. (2009): "Beyond GDP: The Quest for a Measure of Social Welfare," *Journal of Economic Literature*, 47, 1029–75.

HARBERGER, A. C. (1971): "Three Basic Postulates for Applied Welfare Economics: An Interpretive Essay," *Journal of Economic Literature*, 9, 785–97.

HENDERSON, A. (1941): "Consumer's Surplus and the Compensating Variation," *The Review of Economic Studies*, 8, 117–121.

HICKS, J. R. (1942): "Consumers Surplus and Index-Numbers," *The Review of Economic Studies*, 9, 126–137.

LAYARD, P. R. G. AND A. A. WALTERS (1978): *Microeconomic Theory*, New York.

MARSHALL, A. ((1890) 1961): *Principles of Economics*, vol. 2, New York and London: Macmillan, 9 ed.

MCKENZIE, L. (1957): "Demand Theory Without a Utility Index," *The Review of Economic Studies*, 24, 185–189.

SAMUELSON, P. A. AND S. SWAMY (1974): "Invariant Economic Index Numbers and Canonical Duality: Survey and Synthesis," *American Economic Review*, 64, 566–93.

SLESNICK, D. T. (1998): "Empirical Approaches to the Measurement of Welfare," *Journal of Economic Literature*, 36, 2108–2165.

WILLIG, R. D. (1976): "Consumer's Surplus without Apology," *American Economic Review*, 66, 589–97.

# CHAPTER 3

# Theory and Computation

## 3.1 COMPUTATION

Given that the true utility and demand functions are mostly unknown, estimations of welfare changes are based on approximations. The $LV$ and $PV$ approaches do not require utility modeling, and for this reason, they can be estimated by simply using prices and quantities but they do require knowledge of the demand schedule unless price changes can be considered infinitesimal. $LV$ and $PV$ have therefore a computational advantage when compared to the other methods, but we saw that these two approaches represent the boundaries of welfare effect estimations and are, therefore, extreme approximations, particularly when price changes are large.

Below, we first provide a simple approach to the exact estimation of the $LV$ and $PV$ methods using index number theory. We then illustrate estimations of $CS$, $EV$ and $CV$ based on known demand functions (demand functions methods). Next, we propose a simple method based on the own price elasticity (elasticity method). This section is followed by sections on approximation methods including the Taylor, Vartia, Breslaw and Smith and other numerical approximations. The section on Taylor's approximations will also address the questions of how these approximations can be reconciled with the demand functions methods and decomposed into income and substitution effects, two issues that we believe are not entirely clear in the existing literature.

© The Author(s) 2019
A. Araar, P. Verme, *Prices and Welfare*,
https://doi.org/10.1007/978-3-030-17423-1_3

### 3.1.1    Index Numbers

The $LV$ and $PV$ measures are derived from the Laspeyres and Paasche price indexes. For the case of changes in prices and quantities of two products (*general effect*):

$$LV = (p_1^b x_1^a + p_2^b x_2^a) - (p_1^a x_1^a + p_2^a x_2^a) \qquad (3.1)$$

$$PV = (p_1^b x_1^b + p_2^b x_2^b) - (p_1^a x_1^b + p_2^a x_2^b) \qquad (3.2)$$

If we consider only one product and assume no changes in prices or quantities of the other product (*partial effect*), the $LV$ and $PV$ can be simplified to:

$$LV = (p_1^b - p_1^a)x^a = (-)\Delta p_1 x^a \qquad (3.3)$$

$$PV = (p_1^b - p_1^a)x^b = (-)\Delta p_1 x^b \qquad (3.4)$$

which correspond to the formulation provided in the geometric interpretation. The $LV$ formulation is the simplest possible computational case of the welfare effect. It only requires knowledge of initial quantities and changes in prices, information that is known to any practitioner working with micro-data. In all other cases, knowledge or assumptions on the demand schedules are required.

### 3.1.2    Demand Functions

A simple shortcut is to make reasonable assumptions on the utility function and derive the demand curve accordingly. For example, a standard approach in empirical works is to use a utility function based on Cobb–Douglas preferences (see, e.g. Varian 1992):

$$u(x_1, x_2) = x_1^\alpha x_2^{1-\alpha} \qquad (3.5)$$

with the following demand functions given an initial budget constraint $m$:

$$x_1 = \frac{\alpha m}{p_1}; \, x_2 = \frac{(1-\alpha)m}{p_2} \qquad (3.6)$$

Based on these assumptions, we can estimate the $CS$ as the change in the area under the Marshallian demand curve over the change in price. For the change in price of only one product (*partial effect*):

$$CS = \int_{p_1^a}^{p_1^b} \frac{\alpha m}{p_1} dp_1 = \alpha m \ln \frac{p_1^b}{p_1^a} \tag{3.7}$$

In the case of multiple price changes (*general effect*) and considering the simple definition of the $CS$ as the area under the Marshallian demand curve(s), the definition of the $CS$ measurement starts to be incomplete, especially when the demand depends on prices of the other goods, as is the case for the non-homothetic preferences. In this case, different forms of computation may be used, each of them with its specific interpretation. Consider, for example, the following three cases:

*Case A* For each demand function of a given good, estimate the area under the demand curve by keeping the initial prices of the rest of goods equal to their final values:

$$CS = \sum_{i=1}^{n} \int d_i(\mathbf{p}) \Big|_{p_{j\neq i}=p_j^a} dp_i \tag{3.8}$$

*Case B* For each demand function of a given good, estimate the area under the demand curve by keeping a sub-set of the prices of the rest of goods equal to their initial values.

*Case C* For each demand function, integrate over the whole price changes:

$$CS = \sum_{i=1}^{n} \int_1 \int_2 \cdots \int_n d_i(\mathbf{p}) dp_1 dp_2 \ldots dp_n \tag{3.9}$$

Even if case C appears to be the most appropriate to assess the full change in the consumer willingness to pay, case B is the most popular case discussed in the literature even if the $CS$ measurement will depend on the path of price changes. As nicely put by Silberberg (1972):

> One can visualize the path dependence of $\phi$ ($CS$) by noting that if, say, $p_i$ changes, the demand curves for the other commodities begin to shift at the rate $(\partial x_j/\partial p_i)$, $j \neq i$. If, however, some other price $p_j$ changes, the demand for commodity $i$ shifts at the rate $\partial x_i/\partial p_j$. Since these rates are not in general equal, the way in which $p_i$ and $p_j$ are changed—for example, first $p_i$ then $p_j$ or vice-versa—will affect the areas under the demand curves $\int p_i dx_i$ and hence the value of $\phi = \int \sum p_i dx_i$ ($CS$) (p. 944).

It can be noted here that the path independency condition is always satisfied if the preferences are homothetic.

As an example for the Cobb–Douglas preferences, we have that $\int (x_1(\mathbf{p}, m) dp_1 \big|_{p_2=p_2^a} = \int (x_1(\mathbf{p}, m) dp_1 \big|_{p_2=p_2^b}$ and this will be also the case for good 2. Thus, in the case of multiple price changes, the $CS$ is the sum of the changes generated by each price change:

$$CS = \sum_i \alpha_i m \ln \frac{p_i^b}{p_i^a} \tag{3.10}$$

and this sum can be different depending on which price changes first. It can be noted here that the path dependence problem becomes important for the case of multiple price changes (see also Johansson (1987) and Loewenstein (2015)) and when price changes become large.

The estimation of $EV$ and $CV$ based on known demand functions requires solving for these measures an equivalence between *pre* and *post* utility functions. For example, the estimation of $EV$ can be done by solving for $EV$ the following equation:

$$u\left(x_1(p^b, m), x_2(p^b, m)\right) = u\left(x_1(p^a, m + EV), x_2(p^a, m + EV)\right). \tag{3.11}$$

In the case of Cobb–Douglas preferences and multiple changes in prices:

$$\left(\frac{\alpha m}{p_1(1+dp_1)}\right)^{\alpha}\left(\frac{(1-\alpha)m}{p_2(1+dp_2)}\right)^{1-\alpha}$$
$$=\left(\frac{\alpha(m+EV)}{p_1}\right)^{\alpha}\left(\frac{(1-\alpha)(m+EV)}{p_2}\right)^{1-\alpha} \tag{3.12}$$

where $p_k^b = p_k^a + \Delta p_k = p_k^a(1+dp_k)$. By solving for $EV$, we find that:

$$EV = m\left(\frac{1}{(1+dp_1)^{\alpha}(1+dp_2)^{1-\alpha}} - 1\right) \tag{3.13}$$

Similarly, for the $CV$ measurement, one can write:

$$u\left(x_1(p^b, m+CV), x_2(p^b, m+CV)\right) = u\left(x_1(P, m), x_2(P, m)\right) \tag{3.14}$$

which, in the case of Cobb–Douglas preferences and multiple changes in prices, simplifies to:

$$CV = m\left(1 - (1+dp_1)^{\alpha}(1+dp_2)^{1-\alpha}\right) \tag{3.15}$$

A similar approach can be followed by using alternative forms of demand functions, the most popular of which are described in Annex. Note that, by definition, $EV$ and $CV$ are path independent. For the case of non-linear pricing schedule, the $EV$ and $CV$ welfare measurements of the $CD$ model are reported in the Appendix B.1.

### 3.1.3   Elasticity

It is possible to estimate $CS$ with a parsimonious approach that makes use of information on own price elasticity. In some cases, information about own price elasticity is available. For example, one may not know the local demand for gasoline in a particular country, but information on own price elasticity may be largely known in the gasoline sector and roughly similar across countries or at least similar in similar countries. If this information is available and assuming a simple linear demand curve, one can estimate the consumer's surplus as follows:

$$CS = -0.5\,(x + (x + \Delta x))\,\Delta p$$
$$= -0.5\,(x(2 + \eta\Delta p))\,\Delta p$$
$$= -x\Delta p(1 + 0.5\eta\Delta p) \qquad (3.16)$$

where the parameter $\eta$ refers to the global elasticity $(\Delta x/x)/(\Delta p/p)$. The usual assumption when this formula is used is that the global elasticity can be approximated to the local or initial point elasticity, and this implies a moderate change in prices. However, this is often not true. For example, studies on the impact of subsidy reforms often use known point elasticities at market prices of other countries to estimate the $CS$ in a particular country using the formula above. But subsidized prices can be very different from free market prices, sometimes several folds different, and this implies that the local own price elasticity for free market prices cannot be applied to the subsidized price.

There is, however, another method to estimate the global elasticity in the absence of information on the demand curve. Remember that, in the case of homothetic preferences, the uncompensated cross-price elasticities are nil. Assume that all initial prices are normalized to 1 and that we denote the change in price of good 1 by $\Delta p$. The ratio between the percentage of change in quantity and that of price or, in short, the own price elasticity is defined as follows:

$$\eta_1 = \frac{x^b - x^a}{p^b - p^a}\frac{p^a}{x^a} = \frac{\frac{\alpha m}{1+\Delta p} - \frac{\alpha m}{1}}{\Delta p}\frac{1}{\alpha m}. \qquad (3.17)$$

By performing a first simplification, we find that:

$$\eta_1 = \frac{\frac{1}{1+\Delta p} - 1}{\Delta p}, \qquad (3.18)$$

or

$$\eta_1 = \frac{-1}{(1 + \Delta p)} \qquad (3.19)$$

Obviously, for the case of marginal price changes (i.e. $\Delta p \to 0$), we find the traditional value of the uncompensated elasticity, such as $\eta_1 = -1$. Moreover, the traditional decomposition of the compensated elasticity based on the Slutsky equation holds, such that $(\bar{\eta}_1 = \alpha_1 - 1) = (\eta_1 = -1) + (\upsilon = \alpha_1)$. By using this formula, one can then estimate the CS with only knowledge of initial quantities, changes in prices and own price elasticity at free market prices as follows:

$$CS = -x\Delta p(1 - 0.5\Delta p/(1 + \Delta p)) \qquad (3.20)$$

### 3.1.4   Taylor's Approximations

Taylor's approximations are part of a larger family of expansion methods which include Laurent's and Fourier's expansion methods and which can be used to derive numerous Flexible Functional Forms (FFF) such as the normalized quadratic, generalized Leontief or translog functions. We focus here on the Taylor's expansion because of its popularity in economics for the expansion of utility functions and because of its nice properties in relation to the Cobb–Douglas function.

Taylor's approximations are based on Taylor's theorem which states that a function which is $k$-times differentiable can be approximated by a $n$-order polynomial (with $n < k$) by repeatedly differentiating the function around the equilibrium starting point. Applied to $n$-times differentiable utility functions, this theorem allows approximating changes in utility due to price changes with a polynomial made of $n$-order derivatives. The Taylor's approximation becomes more precise with higher-order approximations but also more demanding in terms of information required, which implies a trade-off between simplicity and data requirement.

Hicks (1942) already provided a first quadratic expansion of utility which he used to derive the first *general* formulations of the $CV$ and $EV$ variations as follows:

$$EV = -\sum_k x_k \Delta p_k - 1/2 \sum_{kj} \frac{\partial x_k}{\partial p_j} \Delta p_k \Delta p_j + 1/2 \sum_k x_k \Delta p_k \sum \frac{\partial x_k}{\partial m} \Delta p_k$$

$$(3.21)$$

$$CV = -\sum_k x_k \Delta p_k - 1/2 \sum_{kj} \frac{\partial x_k}{\partial p_j} \Delta p_k \Delta p_j - 1/2 \sum_k x_k \Delta p_k \sum \frac{\partial x_k}{\partial m} \Delta p_k$$

$$(3.22)$$

and showed that the corresponding *partial* (one price change) variations can be written as:

$$EV = -x\Delta p - 1/2\frac{\partial x}{\partial p}(\Delta p)^2 + 1/2x\frac{\partial x}{\partial m}(\Delta p)^2 \qquad (3.23)$$

$$CV = -x\Delta p - 1/2\frac{\partial x}{\partial p}(\Delta p)^2 - 1/2x\frac{\partial x}{\partial m}(\Delta p)^2 \qquad (3.24)$$

which can be reduced to the following if the marginal utility of money is constant ($\frac{\partial x}{\partial m} = 0$):

$$EV = CV = -x\Delta p - 1/2\frac{\partial x}{\partial p}(\Delta p)^2 \qquad (3.25)$$

The latter expression is the Marshallian $CS$ and this implies two important results: (1) In the case of a price change in one product only and with marginal utility of money constant, $CS = EV = CV$, and (2) in other cases, $CV < CS < EV$ always holds.

Starting from the quadratic expansion described above, Hicks (1942) established the following relations:

$$CV - LV = PV - EV = -1/2\sum_{kj} x_{kj}\Delta p_k \Delta p_j \qquad (3.26)$$

which is one half of the total substitution effect induced by a price change and

$$\frac{EV - CV}{LV} = -\sum_k \frac{\partial x_k}{\partial m}\Delta p_k \qquad (3.27)$$

which purely depends on the income effect. From these relations, Hicks (1942) derived that—with changes in prices of only one good and with the exception of the case of an inferior good—$LV < CV < CS, < EV < PV$ as already shown in the geometric interpretation. This result would also normally apply to the case of multiple price changes provided that the $LV$ is larger when the income effect is large.

Moreover, Hicks (1942) shows that—in the case of changes in prices of one item—all measures can be expressed in terms of $LV$ and substitution ($S$) and income ($I$) effects:

$$CV = LV + \frac{1}{2}S \tag{3.28}$$

$$EV = LV + \frac{1}{2}S + I \tag{3.29}$$

$$PV = LV + S + I \tag{3.30}$$

$$CS = LV + \frac{1}{2}S + \frac{1}{2}I \tag{3.31}$$

In essence, the difference between measures is determined by the size of the income and substitution effects, which, in turn, is determined by the shape of the demand function. It should also be noted that these results hold for second-order approximations and quasilinear preferences where the differences between $CV$ and $EV$ and between $LV$ and $PV$ are symmetric with respect to $CS$.

For the case of homothetic preferences and a single price change, we can also generalize the formulae above for $EV$ and $CV$ to higher orders of approximation $o$ so that[1]:

$$EV = \sum_{i=1}^{o} -1^{o} \frac{1}{o!} \left(1 + \frac{\partial x_1}{\partial m}\right)^{(o-1)} x_1 \Delta p_1^{o} \tag{3.32}$$

$$CV = \sum_{i=1}^{o} -1^{o} \frac{1}{o!} \left(1 - \frac{\partial x_1}{\partial m}\right)^{(o-1)} x_1 \Delta p_1^{o} \tag{3.33}$$

Taylor's expansions have been used since the seminal paper by Hicks in numerous contributions, but the interpretation of the terms of approximations of different orders has not been unanimous. Harberger (1971) used a

---

[1] See also Dumagan and Mount (1991) for the general form of preferences and a third order of approximation. Note that, for the rest of the book, higher orders refer to the case of homothetic functions (i.e. $\frac{\partial x_i}{\partial m} = \alpha_i$).

Taylor's expansion of a utility function to describe changes in real incomes and the consumer's surplus as:

$$\Delta u = \sum_k p_k^a \Delta x_k + \frac{1}{2} \sum_k \Delta p_k \Delta x_k + \epsilon \tag{3.34}$$

where the first term on the right-hand side is the first-order change in utility, which is interpreted as the change in real income, the second term is the second-order change in utility, which is interpreted as the change in consumer's surplus, and $\epsilon$ represents higher-order approximations.

Weitzman (1988) provides the same formulation of the Taylor's expansion and, as Harberger, identifies the first term as the change in real income, but equals the second term to the substitution effect. Weitzman (1988) also proves that the sum of the two terms is an exact approximation of the consumer's surplus provided the correct deflator is used and also that the expression can be reduced to the first term for sufficiently small price changes.

This particular expression of the welfare change, even when reduced to the first term, still requires knowledge of the demand function as knowledge of both initial and final quantities are necessary to estimate $\Delta x$. This last problem can be treated using Roy's identity. McKenzie and Pearce (1976), for example, showed that money-metric changes in utility can be measured using a Taylor's series expansion around the initial equilibrium and also noted that money-metric utility is identical to total expenditure when evaluated at the reference prices (see also Slesnick (1998)). In this case, the marginal utility of income is one, and all higher-order income derivatives are zero so that with Taylor's approximation and Roy's identity the change in welfare can be represented as a function of income and price derivatives. In the case of multiple products, the change in utility is as follows:

$$\Delta v(p, m) = -\sum_k x_k \Delta p_k$$

$$-(1/2) \sum_k \sum_j \left( \frac{\partial x_k}{\partial p_j} - x_k \frac{\partial x_j}{\partial m} \right) \Delta p_k \Delta p_j$$

$$+ \left( 1 - \sum_k \frac{\partial x_k}{\partial m} \Delta p_k \right) \Delta m$$

$$+ \epsilon \tag{3.35}$$

where $\epsilon$ represents higher-order terms. Note that when the change in income is nil, the third term disappears and the equation above is reduced to the same formulation proposed by Hicks (1942) for the $EV$ approximation.[2] Moreover, in the case of a price change of only one product and a fixed nominal income $m$, $\Delta p_2 = 0$ and $\Delta m = 0$, the higher first-order terms are nil and the equation above is reduced to the first term $-x\Delta p_1$. Hence, in this particular case, the first-order derivative of the Taylor's expansion is equivalent to the $LV$ measurement.

Another way to see the same result is the following. Let $u(p^b, m)$ be the level of utility after the price change and $m_e$ the equivalent income that generates the same level of utility with $P^a$ such that:

$$u(p^a, m_e) = u(p^b, m) \qquad (3.36)$$

Assuming other prices constant, we can differentiate with respect to $p_1$ and $m_e$ as follows:

$$\frac{\partial u}{\partial m_e} dm_e = \frac{\partial u}{\partial p_1} dp_1. \qquad (3.37)$$

Thus:

$$dm_e = \frac{\partial u}{\partial p_1} \bigg/ \frac{\partial u}{\partial m_e} dp_1. \qquad (3.38)$$

By using the Roy's identity, we find that:

$$dm_e|_{m_e=m} = -x_1 dp_1 \qquad (3.39)$$

This approach is sometimes referred to as the "marginal approach", results in the same $LV$ formula and can be applied to approximate the

---

[2] Note that McKenzie and Pearce (1976) derive the formulae with changes in nominal income, while Hicks considers only the change in prices. For the second term, we have that $\frac{\partial^2 e(p,u)}{\partial p_k \partial p_j} = \frac{\partial h_k(p,u)}{\partial p_j}$. Also, note that the second term is based on the Slutsky equation, so that $\frac{\partial h_k(p,u)}{\partial p_j} = \frac{\partial x_k(p,u)}{\partial p_j} + x_k \frac{\partial x_j}{\partial m}$.

impact of a price change on well-being regardless of the true form of the utility function.[3]

The next question we wish to clarify is how the Taylor expansions of various orders relate to the income and substitution effects. We treat this question separately for the first-order and higher-order polynomials.

**First Order**

It should be obvious by now that the difference between welfare estimation methods relates to the relative difference between the income and substitution effects, which in turn derives from assumptions made on utility and demand functions. It is important therefore to dissect further the role of income and substitution effects and clarify the relation with the Taylor's approximations which, we saw, has been the cause of some confusion in the literature.

Let us start by expressing the change in well-being with the first-order Taylor approximation in the case of multiple products:

$$\Delta v(p, m) = -\sum_i x_i \Delta p_i + \epsilon^1 = v^1(p, m) + \epsilon^1 \qquad (3.40)$$

where $v^1(p, m)$ is the first-term approximation of the welfare change and $\epsilon^1$ the corresponding residual error. In order to explore how this term can be linked to the income and substitution components ($I$ and $S$), we start by recalling the budget constraint:

$$m = p_1 x_1 (p, m(p, u)) + p_2 x_2 (p, m(p, u)) \qquad (3.41)$$

Assume that all initial prices are normalized to one. By differentiating this equation with regard to $p_1$, we find that:

$$\Delta m = 0 = (\Delta x_1 + \Delta x_2) + x_1 \Delta p_1 + \tau^1 \qquad (3.42)$$

or also:

$$v^1(p, m) = (\Delta x_1 + \Delta x_2) + \tau^1 \qquad (3.43)$$

---

[3] See among others Ahmad and Stern (1984, 1991) as well as the works of Newbery (1995), Araar (1998), Creedy (1999, 2001), Yitzhaki and Lewis (1996) and Makdissi and Wodon (2002).

where $\tau^1$ is the error of first-order approximation of the budget constraint. The increase in price of the first good must be compensated by a decrease in the sum of consumed quantities. This finding is important, since it shows that the welfare change depends on the change in quantities. Given that the change in quantity implied by a price change can be decomposed into income and substitution effects ($I = \Delta x_1^I + \Delta x_2^I$ and $S = \Delta x_1^S + \Delta x_2^S$), we can establish the linkage between the Taylor welfare change and the income and substitution effects. Let $u$ denote the direct utility function and $h(p, u)$ the Hicksian demand function. Based on the Slutsky equation, we have that:

$$\frac{\partial x_1\left(p, m(p, u)\right)}{\partial p_1} \Delta p_1 = \left. \frac{\partial h_1\left(p, u\right)}{\partial p_1} \right|_{u=u^a} \Delta p_1 - \frac{\partial x_1\left(p, m(p, u)\right)}{\partial m} x_1 \Delta p_1$$

$$(3.44)$$

The first term on the right-hand side of Eq. 3.44 is related to the substitution effect ($S$), since it expresses the change in quantity when the level of utility is constant, while the second term is related to the income effect. Therefore, it is not entirely correct to argue that the first-order Taylor's approximation is the income effect only. However, one can show that the substitution effect of the first-order Taylor's approximation can be assumed to be very small. Consider the substitution and income effects for the case of two goods and a change in price of the first good:

$$\text{Income effect} = -\left( \frac{\partial x_1\left(p, m(p, u)\right)}{\partial m} + \frac{\partial x_2\left(p, m(p, u)\right)}{\partial m} \right) x_1 \Delta p_1$$

$$(3.45)$$

$$\text{Substitution effect} = \left( \left. \frac{\partial h_1\left(p, u\right)}{\partial p_1} \right|_{u=u^a} + \left. \frac{\partial h_2\left(p, U\right)}{\partial p_1} \right|_{u=u^a} \right) \Delta p_1$$

$$(3.46)$$

The question that may arise now is about the importance of each on the two components with a marginal change in prices. With moderate price changes, we have that[4]:

$$\left.\frac{\partial x_1\,(p, m(p, u))}{\partial m}\right|_{p=1} + \left.\frac{\partial x_2\,(p, m(p, u))}{\partial m}\right|_{p=1} \simeq 1 \qquad (3.47)$$

Thus, the income effect can be simplified to be equal to $-x_1 \Delta p_1$, which is simply the Laspeyres index. The latter is, in turn, an approximation of the $CV$ measurement. This result implies that $S$ must converge to zero so that:

$$\frac{\partial x_1\,(p, m(p, u))}{\partial p_1} \Delta p_1 \simeq -\frac{\partial x_2\,(p, m(p, u))}{\partial p_1} \Delta p_1. \qquad (3.48)$$

In other words, when the consumer re-optimizes the choice after the marginal increase in price of the first good, it is expected that the consumer decreases $x_1$ and increases $x_2$. This adjustment is justified by the *relative* improvement in utility contribution of the per dollar expenditure on good 2. However, the improvement in utility through the substitution process, even if we have an important substitution in quantities, is practically nil. Indeed, with the marginal change in prices, and when we are close to the consumer equilibrium, the latest consumed units of each of the two goods will generate the same level of utility. Thus, the improvement in welfare through the substitution process is practically nil and it can be neglected.

Let $\tilde{S}^o$ and $\tilde{I}^o$ be the approximations of the income and substitution effects according to the $o$ Taylor approximation order. Based on our discussion above, we can conclude what follows:

**Proposition 1** *With the first-order Taylor approximation and small price changes, the substitution effect can be neglected and the first term is a good proxy of the income effect.*

$$v^1(p, m) \approx \tilde{I}^1 + \epsilon_{I^1}$$
$$\tilde{S}^1 \approx 0 \qquad (3.49)$$

---

[4] When initial prices are equal to 1, a marginal increase in income by one unit will change the bought quantities. However, the sum of changes in quantities is equal to 1.

**Proposition 2** *With a first-order Taylor approximation and small price changes $CS$, $CV$ and $EV$ are equal.*

$$\Delta v^1_{CS}(p, m) = \Delta v^1_{CV}(p, m) = \Delta v^1_{EV}(p, m) \qquad (3.50)$$

## Higher Orders

We start from the $CS$ estimation by means of the second-order Taylor approximation in the case of *multiple products changes* (see McKenzie and Pearce (1976)):

$$\Delta v^2_{CS}(p, m) = \sum_i \frac{\partial x_i}{\partial p_i} \Delta p_i - (1/2) \sum_i \sum_j \left( \frac{\partial x_i}{\partial p_j} \right) \Delta p_i \Delta p_j + \epsilon^2 \quad (3.51)$$

For the $CV$ and $EV$ measurements, and as shown by Hicks (1942), we have that:

$$\Delta v^2_{CV}(p, m) = \sum_i \frac{\partial x_i}{\partial p_i} \Delta p_i - (1/2) \sum_i \sum_j \left( \frac{\partial x_i}{\partial p_j} + x_j \frac{\partial x_i}{\partial m} \right) \Delta p_i \Delta p_j + \epsilon^2$$

$$(3.52)$$

$$\Delta v^2_{EV}(p, m) = \sum_i \frac{\partial x_i}{\partial p_i} \Delta p_i - (1/2) \sum_i \sum_j \left( \frac{\partial x_i}{\partial p_j} - x_j \frac{\partial x_i}{\partial m} \right) \Delta p_i \Delta p_j + \epsilon^2$$

$$(3.53)$$

For the case of a *single price change* and with $\lambda = \frac{\partial x_1}{\partial m}$, we have that:

$$\Delta v^2_{CS}(p, m) \simeq \underbrace{-x_1 \Delta p_1 + \frac{1}{2} \lambda x_1 \Delta p^2_i}_{\tilde{i}^2_{CS}} + \underbrace{\frac{1}{2}(1 - \lambda) x_1 \Delta p^2_i}_{\tilde{s}_{CS}{}^2} \qquad (3.54)$$

Similarly, starting from the decomposition of the second order, one can extend this to the highest Taylor orders of approximation ($o$). For the $CS$ measurement and a *single price change*, we can write:

$$\Delta v^o(p,m)_{CS} \simeq \underbrace{\sum_{i=1}^{o} -1^o \frac{1}{o!} \lambda^{(o-1)} x_1 \Delta p_1^o}_{\tilde{I}_{CS}^o} + \underbrace{\sum_{i=2}^{o} -1^o \frac{1}{o!} (1 - \lambda^{(o-1)}) x_1 \Delta p_1^o}_{\tilde{S}_{CS}^o} + \epsilon^o$$

(3.55)

This leads to the following propositions:

**Proposition 3** *With a marginal income change (change by one unit in income), the changes in consumed goods converge to their expenditure shares:* $\lambda \to \alpha$.

The implication of this proposition is important since, with moderate price changes, the impact on well-being—regardless the initial form of consumer preferences—will converge to those based on homothetic preferences (Cobb–Douglas for simplicity).

**Proposition 4** *When the expenditure share of the good is relatively small, the corrected first Taylor approximation term is a good proxy of the income effect, whereas the rest is a good proxy of the substitution effect.*

$$\tilde{I}_{CS}^o = \tilde{I}_{CS}^1 - \frac{\alpha^{(o-1)}}{1 - \alpha^{(o-1)}} \tilde{S}_{CS}^{\tilde{o}}$$

(3.56)

Figure 3.1 compares the sum of changes in quantities with the Taylor approximations of the EV, CV and CS using a Cobb–Douglas model with a utility function of the form $u(x_1, x_2) = x_1^\alpha x_2^{1-\alpha}$, $m = 100$, $p_1 = p_2 = 1$. As shown in the figure, the sum of changes in quantities converges to the usual welfare measurements when price changes are moderate, and the lower is the expenditure share ($\alpha$), the higher is the convergence. Thus, for moderate price changes, and where initial prices are normalized, the change in quantities is close to the change in real expenditures or welfare. This stratagem will help us to check for the relevance of the proposed decomposition in Eq. 3.55. As shown in Fig. 3.2, the three estimates of the

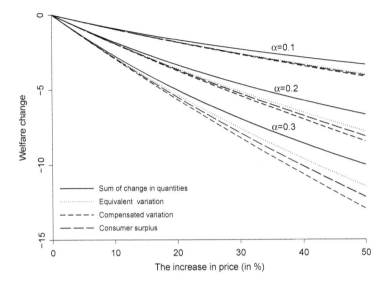

**Fig. 3.1**  Price and welfare changes. Source: Author's calculations

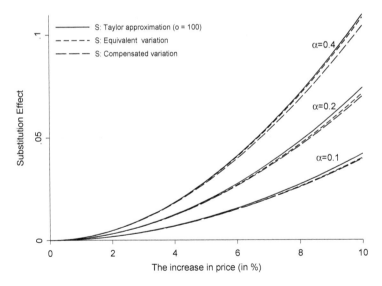

**Fig. 3.2**  Taylor approximation and the substitution effect. Source: Author's calculations

substitution component $S$ converge for small price variations, and this for different values of $\alpha$. With lower values of $\alpha$, the convergence is faster. This confirms the relevance of the new proposed interpretation of the Taylor terms and their relation with the income and substitution effects.[5]

## Convergence and the Cobb–Douglas Function

For the case of the Cobb–Douglas function (i.e. $CS = -\alpha m \log(1 + dp)$), the Taylor approximation of $EV$, $CV$ and $CS$ measurements is a combination of a set of infinite geometric series:

$$EV = x_1 \sum_{i=1}^{o} -1^o \frac{1}{o}(1 + \alpha_1)^{(o-1)} \Delta p_1^o \tag{3.57}$$

$$CV = x_1 \sum_{i=1}^{o} -1^o \frac{1}{o}(1 - \alpha_1)^{(o-1)} \Delta p_1^o \tag{3.58}$$

$$CS = x_1 \sum_{i=1}^{o} -1^o \frac{1}{o} \Delta p_1^o = -x1(ln(1 + \Delta p_1) \text{ where } o \longrightarrow \infty \text{ and } p_1 \longrightarrow 1 \tag{3.59}$$

As we will discover, the Taylor approximations do not converge if the price change exceeds the limit or the radius of convergence ($R$). To find this limit, we have to apply the ratio tests as follows:

$$\frac{1}{R_{EV}} = \left. \frac{\frac{-1^{(o+1)}(1+\alpha)^o}{o+1})}{\frac{-1^o(1+\alpha)^{(o-1)}}{o}} \right|_{o \longrightarrow \infty} = 1 \Rightarrow |R_{EV}| < \frac{1}{1+\alpha} \tag{3.60}$$

---

[5] We have that:

- $S_{CV} = \Delta x_1^S + \Delta x_2^S$ and $C = m(1 + \Delta p_1)^\alpha$
- $\Delta x_1^S = (\alpha C/(1 + \Delta p_1)) - x_1^a$ and $\Delta x_2^S = (1 - \alpha)C/(1) - x_2^a$

Also, we have that:

- $S_{EV} = \Delta x_1^S + \Delta x_2^S$ and $E = m/((1 + \Delta p_1)^\alpha)$
- $\Delta x_1^S = (\alpha E/(1)) - x_1^a$ and $\Delta x_2^S = ((1 - \alpha)E/(1)) - x_2^a$

**Table 3.1**    Cobb–Douglas and the Taylor approximation

| Order ($o$) | Convergent case: $dp_1 = 0.5$ | | Divergent case: $dp_1 = 2.0$ | |
|---|---|---|---|---|
| | Terms $(x_1[-1^o \frac{1}{o}\Delta p_1^o])$ | Cumulative terms | Terms $(x_1[-1^o \frac{1}{o}\Delta p_1^o])$ | Cumulative terms |
| 1 | −15.00 | −15.00 | −60.00 | −60.00 |
| 2 | 3.75 | −11.25 | 60.00 | 0.00 |
| 3 | −1.25 | −12.50 | −80.00 | −80.00 |
| 4 | 0.47 | −12.03 | 120.00 | 40.00 |
| True value | | −12.16 | | −32.96 |

Source: Author's calculations

$$\frac{1}{R_{CV}} = \left.\frac{\frac{-1^{(o+1)}(1-\alpha)^o}{o+1})}{\frac{-1^o(1-\alpha)^{(o-1)}}{o}}\right|_{o \longrightarrow \infty} = 1 \Rightarrow |R_{CV}| < \frac{1}{1-\alpha} \qquad (3.61)$$

$$\frac{1}{R_{CS}} = \left.\frac{\frac{-1^{(o+1)}}{o+1}}{\frac{-1^o}{o}}\right|_{o \longrightarrow \infty} = 1 \Rightarrow |R_{CS}| < 1 \qquad (3.62)$$

For instance, for the $CS$ measurement, if the price change exceeds 100%, the Taylor approximation will give divergent results. To illustrate this, let $U = x_1^{0.3}x_2^{0.7}$, $m = 100$ and two cases of price change, as shown in Table 3.1. As we can observe, the additional correction terms become large when the change in price is outside the range of convergence $[-1, 1]$. In the divergent case ($dp_1 = 2.0$), we can have unexpected results such as an increase in well-being with the fourth order of approximation.

Starting from the fact that the demand function can be modeled and estimated with only the observed market information, the question that may raise is: is it enough to use the Marshallian demand function to estimate the $CV$ and the $EV$ measurements? The pioneering work that has addressed this question is that of Hausman (1980). The author defines the exact functional form of the $CV$ ($EV$) measurement for selected Marshallian demand functions. Later works such as that of Vartia (1983) develop instead numerical general approaches to estimate the $CV$ and $EV$ measurements that can be applied in the context of any functional form of demand.

### 3.1.5    *Vartia's Approximation*

Vartia (1983) proposed a different approach to the measurement of welfare changes. Instead of assuming *ex-ante* a utility function or trying to derive welfare changes from the Taylor's expansion of an unknown utility function, Vartia proposes to work backward, starting from a known demand function and deriving from this function the utility change. This approach is based on the theory of revealed preferences and is the opposite of the approach where we first assume a utility function and derive from this function the demand schedules.

Vartia derives first the conditions that relate a demand function $h(.)$ to the indirect utility function $V(p, C)$ and based on these conditions derives the first-order differential equation in the cost (expenditure or money income) function $C(.)$:

$$\frac{\partial C(t)}{\partial t} = \sum h_k(p(t), C(t)) \frac{\partial p_i(t)}{\partial t} \tag{3.63}$$

where $t$ refers to the number of the iteration. With knowledge of the demand function, it is possible to derive $x$ iteratively and estimate $\Delta C$.[6] Hence, the $CV$ can be expressed in terms of sum of marginal changes over a known demand function.

$$CV = 1/2 \sum_t \sum_k (x_k(p^t, m^t) + x_k(p^{t-1}, m^{t-1}, ))(p_k^t - p_k^{t-1})) \tag{3.64}$$

For the $CV$ measurement, we have that $p^{t=0} = p^a$ is the initial price and $p^{t=n} = p^b$ is the final price when the number of iterates is $n$ and that $p^t - p^{t-1} = dp/n$. The Vartia algorithm is reversible and this enables to estimate the $EV$ at price $p_t$ as:

$$EV = 1/2 \sum_t \sum_k (x_k(p^{n-t}, m^t) + x_k(p^{n-(t-1)}, m^{t-1}, ))(p_k^{n-t} - p_k^{n-(t-1)})) \tag{3.65}$$

and $m^t = \hat{m}^{t-1}$. Note that $p_k^{n-t}$ for $t = 0$ is simply the price of good $k$ in the final period.

---

[6] See Bacon (1995) for a simple spreadsheet approach to the use of the Vartia's method.

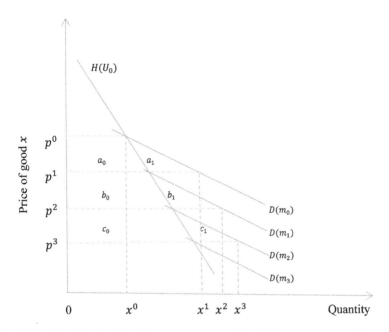

**Fig. 3.3** The Vartia algorithm to compute the $CV$ measurement. Source: Author's calculations

Below, we use an illustration from Chen (2009) to introduce the Vartia algorithm and show how to estimate the compensated income $m^c$ (Fig. 3.3). We assume that the price decreases from $p^0$ to $p^3$. The compensated income at $p^1$ is the initial income plus the area $a_0$. However, this latter is simply approximated to $a_0 + a_1$ using intermediately the Marshallian demand function for the estimation. After this first iteration, we move to the second iteration to assess the compensated income at $p_2$. This is based on the estimated $m_1$ plus the $CV$ from $p_1$ to $p_2$ which is approximated to the area $b_0 + b_1$. The same procedure is repeated to assess $m_3$ at price $p^3$. At the end, the compensated income ($m_3$) at $p^3$ is equal to $(m + (a_0 + b_0 + c_0) + (a_1 + b_1 + c_1))$. Of course, the error term $(a_1 + b_1 + c_1)$ will converge to zero when the number of iterations is high and the price change in each iteration becomes infinitesimal. The empirical part will show a computation of this method.

To illustrate the point of increasing precision of the Vartia algorithm with increasing iterations, we report in Table 3.2 the estimate of the $CV$ and $EV$ measurements for the case of Cobb–Douglas ($U = x_1^{0.3} x_2^{0.7}$)

**Table 3.2** CV and EV estimations with Vartia's algorithm

| $n$ | $CV$ | $EV$ |
|---|---|---|
| 10 | −8.3390394 | 7.5393912 |
| 100 | −8.2046317 | 7.5653872 |
| 1000 | −8.1905470 | 7.5687568 |
| 10000 | −8.1891321 | 7.5691015 |
| 100000 | −8.1889906 | 7.5691361 |
| True value | −8.1889749 | −7.5691399 |

Source: Author's calculations

preferences and a change in the price of good 1 from 1 to 1.3. As shown in Table 3.2, starting from 100 iterations, the error measurement becomes very small.

### 3.1.6    Breslaw and Smith's Approximation

The method of computation proposed by Breslaw and Smith (1995) is based on the second-order Taylor approximation, proposed by McKenzie and Pearce (1976). In matrix form, the compensated income at step $t$ is evaluated as follows:

$$C_{t+1} = C_t + x(p_t, C_t)' \Delta p_{t+1} + \Delta p'_{t+1} \varphi_t \Delta p_{t+1} \qquad (3.66)$$

where $C_0 = m$, the Slutsky matrix element is $\varphi_t[i, j] = \frac{\partial x_{i,t}}{\partial p_j} - x_{i,t} \frac{\partial x_{j,t}}{\partial C}$ and $\Delta p_{t+1} = p_{t+1} - p_t$. As indicated in Breslaw and Smith (1995), the estimation of the $EV$ is based on an algorithm which is quite similar to that of the $CV$ such as $EV(p^a \to p^b) = -CV(p^b \to p^a)$.[7]

### 3.1.7    The Ordinary Differential Equations Methods

Welfare change measurements can be expressed as an integral of ordinary differential equations (ODE). It is assumed that the welfare measurement function, like $CV$ or $EV$, is continuous and first order differentiable with respect to the price (i.e. $w' = f(p, m)$). It follows that the integral

---

[7] Breslaw and Smith (1995) claim that their algorithm converges faster than the Vartia's algorithm, while the work done by Sun and Xie (2013) shows the superiority of the latter. We tested the performance of the two algorithms both programmed in Stata, and we found the Breslaw and Smith algorithm to be faster.

of the function $f(p, m)$ between $p^a$ and $p^b$ is equal to the welfare change. Mathematics offers numerous numerical methods mostly based on an adaptive process of estimation with successive steps of evaluation. Economists are generally less familiar with these approaches while they use extensively the Taylor approximation approach, even with large changes in independent variables (price in our case). However, the Taylor approach can fail to evaluate accurately the function when the order of approximation is low or when the price change is large.

Numerical approximations can be helpful for several reasons. First, they enable to overcome the integrability problem, since they use an adaptive process and evaluate the impact for successive small price changes. This also makes the substitution effect practically nil given the small price change in each step. Second, they enable to overcome the problem of higher-order derivatives, especially in the case of complex functional forms. This simplification derives from using the first derivative to approximate higher-order derivatives. Third, compared to the Taylor approximation approach, this method is the most relevant in the case of large price changes (see Lim (2012) for an extensive review of these methods). As an example, we introduce two popular numerical approximation methods: the Euler method and the Fourth Runge and Kutta method.

The **Euler method** can be viewed as a solution of first-order ordinary differential equations (ODE). Formally, it is based on the following main function:

$$w_{i+1} = w_i + hf(p_i, w_i) \tag{3.67}$$

where $h = (p^b - p^a)/n$; $p_i = p^a + ih$ and $p_n = p^b$.

The **Fourth Runge and Kutta method** (RK4 in short) is based implicitly on the fourth Taylor approximation:

$$w_{i+1} = w_i + (1/6)h(k_{i,1} + 2k_{i,2} + 2k_{i,3} + k_{i,4}) \tag{3.68}$$

where

$$k_{i,1} = f(p_i, w_i)$$
$$k_{i,2} = f(p_{i+0.5h}, w_i + 0.5k_{i,1}h)$$
$$k_{i,3} = f(p_{i+0.5h}, w_i + 0.5k_{i,2}h)$$
$$k_{i,4} = f(p_{i+h}, w_i + k_{i,3}h)$$

To illustrate how these numerical methods are relevant for our purpose, we return to our simple Cobb–Douglas example where $w$ can be the compensated or equivalent income. Remember that $\frac{\partial v(p,m)}{\partial p} = -x(p,m)$. Then, for the case of the CD function, we have that $f(p, w) = -\alpha w/p$. As an example, Table 3.3 shows the computation of the two methods using as parameters $\alpha=0.3$, $p^a=1$, $p^b = 1.3$, $h=0.25$ and $m_0 = w_0=100$. The RK4 provides a better approximation of the true values when compared with the Euler method, but it requires the modeling of preferences or at least the Marshallian demand functions similarly to the Vartia (1983) or the Breslaw and Smith (1995) algorithms.

### 3.1.8    Relational Approach

Studies on welfare measures have established a number of algebraic relations between these measures. For example, we showed that Hicks (1942) found that $CS$, $EV$ and $CV$ could be derived from $LV$, $I$ and $S$ so that knowledge of the latter three measures is sufficient to derive the other three measures (under certain assumptions). Chipman and Moore (1980) have also shown that the $CV$ and $EV$ can be derived from the $CS$ as follows:

$$CV = (1 - e^{-CS/m})m \tag{3.69}$$

$$EV = (e^{CS/m} - 1)m \tag{3.70}$$

which is useful in that, for example, one could derive $CS$ using the elasticity method or the Taylor's approximation described and then derive $CV$ and $EV$ from the formulae above. Moreover, one can also reverse the Hicks (1942) equations to find $LV$ or reverse the Chipman and Moore (1980) equations to find $CS$. These relations multiply the possibilities of estimating all five welfare measures under limited information.

Other established relations between measures that help to set the relative boundaries of these measures are Willig (1976) and Cory et al. (1981).

**Table 3.3**  Euler and RK4 method simulations

| Step : i | $p_i = p^a + h * i$ | EV | | | $p_i = p^b - h * i$ | CV | | |
|---|---|---|---|---|---|---|---|---|
| | | Euler | RK4 | True value | | Euler | RK4 | True value |
| 0 | 1.00 | 0.000 | 0.000 | 0.000 | 2.00 | 0.000 | 0.000 | |
| 1 | 1.25 | −5.613 | −6.475 | −6.475 | 1.75 | 4.461 | 4.085 | |
| 2 | 1.50 | −10.041 | −11.453 | −11.453 | 1.50 | 9.911 | 9.008 | |
| 3 | 1.75 | −13.664 | −15.455 | −15.455 | 1.25 | 16.818 | 15.131 | |
| 4 | 2.00 | −16.710 | −18.775 | −18.775 | 1.00 | 26.048 | 23.091 | 23.114 |

Source: Author's calculations

Willig (1976) has developed the following rule of thumb in the case of a single price change. If $|\eta/2m| \leq 0.05|$ and $CS/m \leq 0.90$, then:

$$\frac{\underline{\eta}|CS|}{2m} \leq \frac{CV - CS}{|CS|} \leq \frac{\bar{\eta}|CS|}{2m}$$

$$\frac{\underline{\eta}|CS|}{2m} \leq \frac{CS - EV}{|CS|} \leq \frac{\bar{\eta}|CS|}{2m} \qquad (3.71)$$

where $\underline{\eta}$ and $\bar{\eta}$ refer to the minimum and the maximum income elasticity within the range of price change. The relative importance between $CS$ and $m$ will depend on the extent of price change and the expenditure share. Thus, one can derive that $CV$, $EV$ and $CS$ tend to converge if the expenditure share is small or in the case of moderate price changes.

Based on the $LV$ and $PV$ methods, Cory et al. (1981) provide interesting rules under the assumption on linearity of demand curves. If we denote the error term by $\lambda$, we have that:

$$\frac{CS - LV}{|CS|} \leq \lambda \text{ if } \frac{\Delta x}{x} \leq \frac{2\lambda}{1 - \lambda}$$

$$\frac{PV - CS}{|CS|} \leq \lambda \text{ if } \frac{\Delta x}{x} \leq \frac{2\lambda}{1 - \lambda} \qquad (3.72)$$

Therefore, the lower is the price elasticity, and the change in quantity, the lower is the error of approximation. In the extreme case where the price elasticity is nil, $CS = LV = PV$.

## REFERENCES

AHMAD, E. AND N. STERN (1984): "The Theory of Reform and Indian Indirect Taxes," *Journal of Public Economics*, 25, 259–98.

AHMAD, E. AND N. H. STERN (1991): *The Theory and Practice of Tax Reform in Developing Countries*, Cambridge.

ARAAR, A. (1998): "Les mesures d'inégalité relative et les fonctions de bien-être social, ch. 3, in, Le bien-être des ménages et la transition économique en Pologne," Ph.d. thesis, Université Laval.

BACON, R. (1995): "Measurement of Welfare Changes Caused by Large Price Shifts," World Bank Discussion Paper 273, World Bank.

BRESLAW, J. A. AND J. B. SMITH (1995): "A Simple and Efficient Method for Estimating the Magnitude and Precision of Welfare Changes," *Journal of Applied Econometrics*, 10, 313–27.

CHEN, X. (2009): "Consumer Surplus in Practice," Tech. rep., Department of Applied Economics and Management, Cornell University.

CHIPMAN, J. S. AND J. C. MOORE (1980): "Compensating Variation, Consumer's Surplus, and Welfare," *The American Economic Review*, 70, 933–949.

CORY, D. C., R. L. GUM, W. E. MARTIN, AND R. F. BROKKEN (1981): "Simplified Measurement of Consumer Welfare Change," *American Journal of Agricultural Economics*, 63, 715–717.

CREEDY, J. (1999): "Marginal Indirect Tax Reform in Australia," *Economic Analysis and Policy*, 29, 1–14.

——— (2001): "Indirect Tax Reform and the Role of Exemptions," *Fiscal Studies*, 22, 457–86.

DUMAGAN, J. C. AND T. D. MOUNT (1991): "Measuring Hicksian Welfare Changes from Marshallian Demand Functions," Research Bulletins 123112, Cornell University, Department of Applied Economics and Management.

HARBERGER, A. C. (1971): "Three Basic Postulates for Applied Welfare Economics: An Interpretive Essay," *Journal of Economic Literature*, 9, 785–97.

HAUSMAN, J. (1980): "Exact Consumer Surplus and Deadweight Loss," *AER*, 71, 662–76.

HICKS, J. R. (1942): "Consumers Surplus and Index-Numbers," *The Review of Economic Studies*, 9, 126–137.

JOHANSSON, P.-O. (1987): *The Economic Theory and Measurement of Environmental Benefits*, no. 9780521348102 in Cambridge Books, Cambridge University Press.

LIM, S. J. (2012): "The numerical approximation for the integrability problem and the measure of welfare changes, and its applications," Ph.D. thesis, University of Kansas.

LOEWENSTEIN, W. (2015): "The Path Dependency Problem of Marshallian Consumer's Surplus Revisited," SSRN: https://ssrn.com/abstract=2469207 or http://dx.doi.org/10.2139/ssrn.2469207.

MAKDISSI, P. AND Q. WODON (2002): "Consumption Dominance Curves: Testing for the Impact of Indirect Tax Reforms on Poverty," *Economics Letters*, 75, 227–35.

MCKENZIE, G. AND I. PEARCE (1976): "Exact Measures of Welfare and the Cost of Living," *The Review of Economic Studies*, 43, 465–468.

NEWBERY, D. (1995): "The Distributional Impact of Price Changes in Hungary and the United Kingdom," *Economic Journal*, 105, 847–63.

SILBERBERG, E. (1972): "Duality and the many consumer's surpluses." The American Economic Review 62(December), 942–952.

SLESNICK, D. T. (1998): "Empirical Approaches to the Measurement of Welfare," *Journal of Economic Literature*, 36, 2108–2165.

SUN, Z. AND Y. XIE (2013): "Error Analysis and Comparison of Two Algorithms Measuring Compensated Income," *Computational Economics*, 42, 433–452.

VARIAN, H. R. (1992): "Microeconomic Analysis", New York: W.W. Norton & Company, 3rd ed.

VARTIA, Y. O. (1983): "Efficient Methods of Measuring Welfare Change and Compensated Income in Terms of Ordinary Demand Functions," *Econometrica*, 51, 79–98.

WEITZMAN, M. L. (1988): "Consumer's Surplus as an Exact Approximation When Prices Are Appropriately Deflated," *The Quarterly Journal of Economics*, 103, 543–53.

WILLIG, R. D. (1976): "Consumer's Surplus without Apology," *American Economic Review*, 66, 589–97.

YITZHAKI, S. AND J. LEWIS (1996): "Guidelines on Searching for a Dalton-Improving Tax Reform: An Illustration with Data from Indonesia," *The World Bank Economic Review*, 10, 541–562.

# CHAPTER 4

# Empirical Applications

## 4.1 Applications

In empirical works, there is clearly a trade-off between the degree of approximation of true measures of welfare and the degree of complexity in estimating these same measures. Ideally, one would want to use the simplest of the measures proposed and the most parsimonious in terms of data requirements. But, in some cases, this simplicity comes with a cost in terms of estimation errors. The discussion provided thus far on the various measures proposed indicated that the critical factor in making a choice between welfare methods and approximation strategies is the size of the price change which has implications on the size of the income and substitution effects. For small price changes, some of the parameters used by the various welfare measures converge to zero and this makes simple measures accurate. For large price changes, key parameters do not converge to zero and this makes simple measures inaccurate. Therefore, the question we want to address now is how we can determine what is a small or large price change and what are the best strategies to follow in empirical research under the two scenarios.

The review of the estimation methods and approximation strategies proposed revealed that there is only one formulation of the welfare effects that does not require any modeling of preferences or demand schedules and that requires the least amount of information. This is the $-x\Delta p$ formula also labeled as the "marginal approach", which is the $LV$ method or,

© The Author(s) 2019
A. Araar, P. Verme, *Prices and Welfare*,
https://doi.org/10.1007/978-3-030-17423-1_4

equivalently, the $CS$, $EV$ or $CV$ methods under certain restrictions as already discussed. It is therefore instructive to discuss the potential error size of this formula before undertaking more complex approximations of the welfare effect that invariably lead to demand modeling of some sort.

The question of the error size is, of course, non-trivial. If utility and demand functions were known, then changes in quantities due to price changes could be calculated with precision and one could judge which of the estimation methods come closer to reality. But if utility and demand are latent functions largely unknown to the observer, then we don't have a benchmark to measure the true error size. In this case—which is the case for most analysts—the only tests we can conduct are about the difference between estimation methods for different price increases. This is what we do in this section treating separately individual and social welfare. Recall that we treat social welfare as a simple non-weighted aggregation of individual welfare. Hence, the question of small and large price changes is treated under individual welfare only, while we focus on the question of comparing distributions under the social welfare section.

### 4.1.1    Individual Welfare

**Small Price Variations**

For small price variations, the optimal strategy is to use $LV$ for two good reasons. One is that this is the measure that requires the least information to be computed, and the second is that estimations produced by other measures converge to the $LV$ measure for small price variations. The question we want to address here is: what is "small"? What price variations are small enough to make $LV$ a viable tool? Or, at what point $LV$ and other measures start to diverge significantly? We consider the case of a single price change or multiple price changes and the role of the Cobb–Douglas parameter "alpha".

*Single Price Change* We can start with an illustrative example comparing $LV$ estimates with $EV$ estimates derived from Cobb–Douglas preferences in the case of a price change of only one product. We assume that the "true" utility is defined with Cobb–Douglas preferences with $U(x_1, x_2) = x_1^{\alpha} x_2^{1-\alpha}$ and $\alpha = 0.3$. Assume also that initially we have income $m = 100$, and prices $p_1 = p_2 = 1$. Figures 4.1 and 4.2 show respectively the impact on welfare and the error size estimated for price increases between 0 and 50 percent.

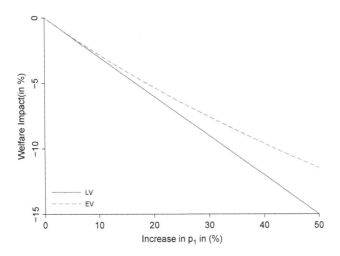

**Fig. 4.1** Well-being and price changes. Source: Author's calculations

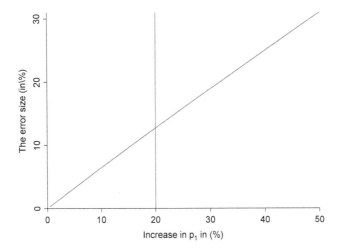

**Fig. 4.2** Error size and price change. Source: Author's calculations

It is shown that $LV$ provides similar estimates to $EV$ up to a price increase of around 10 percent, while estimates diverge by about 12 percent for price increases around 20 percent (Fig. 4.1). We can also estimate the percentage error between the two measures—$|(LV - EV)/EV|$ (Fig. 4.2)—and this shows that the error is about 6 percent for price increases of about 10 percent and doubles to around 12 percent for price increases around 20 percent. It is also visible that the error is a linear function of the price increase. As already discussed, the marginal approach $LV$ tends to overestimate the negative impact on welfare as compared to other measures. This is due to the fact that the marginal approach essentially captures the income effect but not the substitution effect.

The bias illustrated in Fig. 4.2 is also discussed by Banks et al. (1996). Using European data, they find a bias between 5 and 10 percentage points with a price change ranging from 10 to 20 percent. They also confirm the negligible impact when price changes are below 10 percent.

Using the same setting based on Cobb–Douglas preferences, we can now extend comparisons to the other welfare measures considered. Note that the income effect is approximated by $LV$, while the substitution effect is given by:

$$S = \left( \frac{\partial h_1 (p, u)}{\partial p_1} \bigg|_{u=u^a} + \frac{\partial h_2 (p, u)}{\partial p_1} \bigg|_{u=u^a} \right) \Delta p_1$$

$$= \left( \frac{\alpha(\alpha - 1)}{p_1^2} + \frac{\alpha(1 - \alpha)}{p_1 p_2} \right) m \Delta p_1 \tag{4.1}$$

In Fig. 4.3, we show the estimates of the different measurements as well as the income and substitution effects. First, we can see that $|LV| > |EV| > |CS| > |CV| > |PV|$ holds as found in the theoretical part. Second, the total effect $(I + S)$ converges to the $CS$ measurement. Note that, by construction, the first-order Taylor approximation $(LV)$ implies nil impact of the interaction effect. Further, for moderate price changes, the $CS$ measurement is also a good proxy of the $CV$ and $EV$ measurements given that the utility or real income earned through the substitution effect is negligible. It is also evident that divergence across methods occurs around price increases of 10 percent and above.

In the case discussed above, we only considered changes in prices in one of the two goods considered. By construction, the first-order marginal

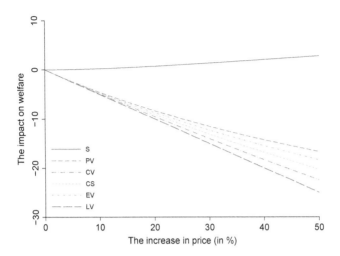

**Fig. 4.3** Price and welfare changes and the substitution effect. Source: Author's calculations

approach avoids the inclusion of the iteration effect (i.e. the impact of cross-price changes $dp_i\, dp_j$). Therefore, if one wishes to estimate multiple price changes with the marginal approach, this would be done by simply adding up the welfare effect for each product so that the total impact would amount to $\Delta W = -\sum_{i=1}^{I} x_i dp_i$. However, this is clearly an overestimation of the true effect. That is because the increase in price of a good increases demand for substitute goods and, consequently, the price of the substitutes. Note also that, assuming homothetic preferences, the change in consumer surplus takes an additive form across goods (the non-compensated cross-elasticities are nil) so that $\Delta CS = -\sum_{i=1}^{I} x_i \log(1 + dp_i)$.

*Multiple Price Changes* We now consider the case of simultaneous price changes across multiple products. In addition to the increase in $dp_1$, assume an increase in the price of good 2: $dp_2 = 0.5 dp_1$. As it can be observed by comparing the results of Fig. 4.4 with those of 4.3, the substitution effect is reduced significantly after the increase in price of the second good. This is explained by the reduction in the substitution effect due to the simultaneous increase in prices.

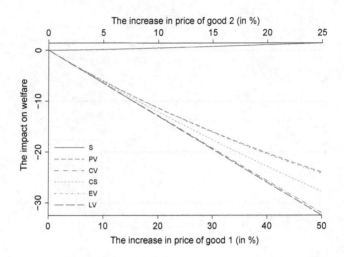

**Fig. 4.4** Price and welfare changes (multiple price changes). Source: Author's calculations

*The Role of the Product's Share ($\alpha$)* Differences between estimation methods based on Cobb–Douglas preferences also depend on the parameters used. The exponential "alpha" can take any value between 0 and 1. To test how different estimation measures spread apart as prices increase and under different alpha parameters, we compare in Fig. 4.5 the five measures using $\alpha = 0.1$ and $\alpha = 0.5$. As expected, results show that for low values of alpha the different estimation methods are very close up to 50 percent price increases while they diverge substantially for high values of alpha already around price increases of 20 percent. Values of alpha are set by the researcher based on notions that may come from the literature or from data. The important lesson to keep in mind here is that the higher the alpha parameter, the higher the divergence between estimation methods so that with very low alpha one may still consider to use the $LV$ approach, even with price increases as large as 50 percent.

This section has shown that the answer to the question of what is a small price change that would sanction the use of $LV$ as the preferred measure is not straightforward. With a given Cobb–Douglas demand function, it depends on whether we model one or more price changes and on the size of $\alpha$ in addition to the size of the price change.

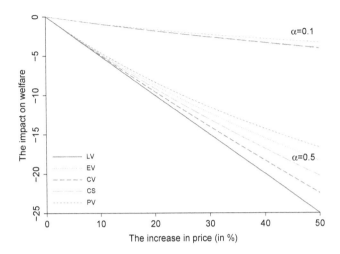

**Fig. 4.5** Price, expenditure share and welfare changes. Source: Author's calculations

### Large Price Variations

For large price variations, the choice between measures becomes important as these measures diverge significantly in estimating the welfare effect of a price change. This also means that it is important to evaluate the role of the choice of demand function and the choice of alternative approximation methods such as Hicks's or Taylor's methods. This is what we explore in this section.

*Demand Systems* So far, we used a Cobb–Douglas demand framework to assess differences across measures, but results and conclusions may have been different had we used different forms of demand functions. To address this question, we compare $EV$ estimations derived from a Cobb–Douglas model with the ones derived from other popular demand systems including the Linear Expenditure System (LES), the Almost Ideal Demand System (AIDS), the Quadratic Almost Ideal Demand System (QUAIDS) and the Exact Affine Stone Index (EASI) with a six-order polynomial expansion.[1] As a benchmark, we also report results for $LV$.

---

[1] See Deaton and Muellbauer (1980), Banks et al. (1997), Lewbel and Pendakur (2009) and Appendix A.1.

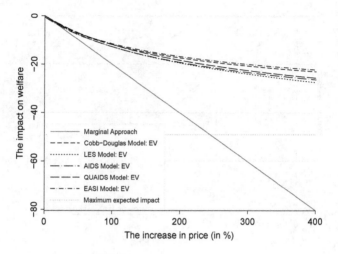

**Fig. 4.6** Restricted information and welfare measurement. Source: Author's calculations

For this purpose, we use data from the 1987/88 *Nationwide Food Consumption Survey*, which is conducted by the United States Department of Agriculture. Demands for four categories of food are estimated: meats, fruits and vegetables, breads and cereals, and miscellaneous. In Fig. 4.6, we assess the impact of a potential increase in the price of meats. Note that for the Cobb–Douglas model, the compensated own-price and cross-price elasticities for good $i$ are $(\alpha_i - 1)$ and $\alpha_j$ respectively ($\alpha_l$ is the expenditure share of good $l$).[2] Of course, this may—slightly—underestimate the welfare effect because of the overestimation of the substitution effect component. This is also confirmed by the low estimated compensated cross-elasticities with the QUAIDS model compared to those of the Cobb–Douglas model.

Figure 4.6 shows that the marginal approach (LV) overestimates the impact on welfare as compared to all $EV$ estimations irrespective of the demand model used. For instance, when the price of meat quadruples, the impact is $-80$ USD, which is even higher than the maximum reasonable impact not exceeding total expenditures (less than 50 USD on average), in the case of perfect complement goods and non-substitutable goods. Overall, the demand models show a clear ranking with the Cobb–Douglas

---

[2] See, for instance, Ramskov and Munksgaard (2001).

model providing smaller estimates as compared to the EASI, QUAIDS, AIDS and LES models. All models provide very close estimates diverging of a few percentage points only for very high price changes. QUAIDS, AIDS and LES are particularly close even at price increases of 400 percent.

We shall conclude that the choice of the demand system is not a major discriminatory factor in determining differences in welfare estimations and that the use of the simple Cobb–Douglas model is reasonable even for very high price increases with the caveat that it may underestimate the welfare effect as compared to other more sophisticated demand models. However, given the simplicity of the Cobb–Douglas model and its nice properties in relation to the share of goods consumed over total consumption, to its capacity to estimate easily all measures of welfare change and in relation to the Taylor approximations, this model remains, in our view, the model of choice.

*Other Approximation Methods* The next question we want to address is how other estimation methods including the elasticity method and Hicks or Taylor approximations of various degrees compare to the Cobb–Douglas demand method. We start by comparing the Cobb–Douglas method with the elasticity and Taylor approximations (Fig. 4.7). Consider

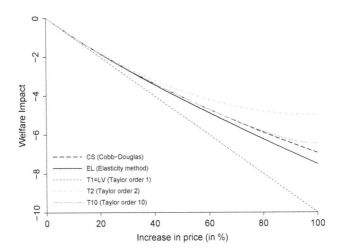

**Fig. 4.7** Cobb–Douglas vs. elasticity and Taylor methods. Source: Author's calculations

the following example. Suppose that the true preferences are Cobb–Douglas and that we consider as "errors" the differences from these estimates. With initial prices normalized to one, we have $CS = -m\alpha \log(1 + dp_1)$. Now assume that the price of the first good doubles and that the global elasticity of the linear demand curve is equal to $-0.5$. Based on the approximation of Eq. 3.16, we find that $CS = -22.5$ whereas the true (Cobb–Douglas) value is equal to $CS = -20.79$. This error is evidently explained by the assumption of the linear demand curve, and it can become quite large as shown in Fig. 4.7. We can also see that estimates made with the elasticity method are rather close to the Cobb–Douglas demand method up to 100 percent price increases. The error size can be better appreciated in Fig. 4.8. The elasticity method results in a rather good approximation of the Taylor's higher-order estimate and converges to this value around price increases of 100%. Hence, the elasticity method can be considered as a viable simple alternative to Cobb–Douglas preferences up to very large price changes.

We now test the performance of the Hicks approximations as compared to the Cobb–Douglas demand function using CV and EV measures (Fig. 4.9). The Cobb–Douglas model is $u = x_1^{0.3} x_2^{0.7}$, $p_1^a = p_2^a = 1$ and $m = 100$. For moderate price variations (say up to 20 percent), the second-

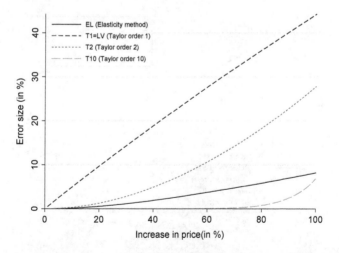

**Fig. 4.8** Cobb–Douglas vs. elasticity and Taylor methods (error size). Source: Author's calculations

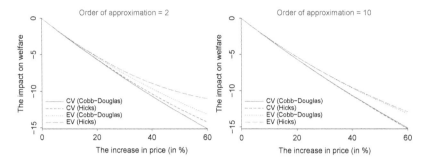

**Fig. 4.9** Taylor approximation and welfare change. Source: Author's calculations

order approximation proposed by Hicks (1942) is enough to approximate the Cobb–Douglas $CV$ and $EV$ measurements. For large price variations, we clearly need to use higher-order approximations. As shown, in the right-hand panel of the figure, a tenth degree order of approximation results in estimates that are very close to those provided by the Cobb–Douglas demand function, but this is true only for price variations up to about 20%. Hence, Taylor's approximations, even of high degree, diverge from Cobb–Douglas estimations early on the scale of possible price increases.

### A Choice Tool for Practitioners

We are now in a position to provide more precise indications on choices of measures and computational methods for practitioners. Table 4.1 summarizes welfare measures, computational methods and minimum requirements for all measures we considered in this book. Using these measures, we can simulate alternative sets of price changes and compare results. For all estimations that require modeling preferences, we use a Cobb–Douglas function with four parameters described as:

$$u(x_1, x_2) = x_1^{0.3} x_2^{0.1} x_3^{0.2} x_4^{0.4} \tag{4.2}$$

This represents a utility function of an individual or household with a four-product consumption basket and the relative weight of each product represented by the exponential. We consider six alternative scenarios for small, medium and large price increases. Scenarios 1–3 consider only one price change, while scenarios 4–6 consider multiple price changes.

**Table 4.1**  Summary of welfare measure, computation methods and functional requirements

| Welfare change measurement | Equation | Requirements |
|---|---|---|
| LV | 3.3 | Initial quantities/expenditures |
| PV | 3.4 | Marshallian demand function |
| CS: True value | 3.7 | Marshallian demand function |
| CS: Elasticity approximation | 3.20 | Initial quantities/expenditures |
| CS: TAYLOR_(order = 2) | 3.54 | Marshallian demand function |
| CS: TAYLOR_(order = 3) | 3.59 | Marshallian demand function |
| EV: True value | 3.13 | Indirect utility function |
| EV: Taylor (order = 2) | 3.53 | Marshallian demand function |
| EV: Taylor (order = 3) | 3.59 | Marshallian demand function |
| EV: Vartia (10 iterations) | 3.65 | Marshallian demand function |
| EV: Breslaw and Smith (10 iterations) | 3.66 | Marshallian demand function/numerical derivatives |
| EV: Euler (10 iterations) | 3.67 | first-order derivative of the welfare function |
| EV: RK4 (10 iterations) | 3.68 | first-order derivative of the welfare function |
| CV: True value | 3.15 | Indirect utility function |
| CV: Taylor (order = 2) | 3.52 | Marshallian demand function |
| CV: Taylor (order = 3) | 3.58 | Marshallian demand function |
| CV: Vartia (10 iterations) | 3.64 | Marshallian demand function |
| CV: Breslaw and Smith (10 iterations) | 3.66 | Marshallian demand function/numerical derivatives |
| CV: Euler (10 iterations) | 3.67 | first-order derivative of the welfare function |
| CV: RK4 (10 iterations) | 3.68 | first-order derivative of the welfare function |

Source: Author's calculations

Price changes for the four products considered are reported at the top of Table 4.2. For all simulations, we consider household expenditure $m = 100$. Results are shown in Table 4.2 and can be summarized as follows:

- The difference between measures is small for small price variations (S1 and S4), whether it is one or more price variations.
- The difference between measures becomes large for medium price variations (S2 and S5). Relative to the initial expenditure $m = 100$, the difference between the lower and upper bounds (PV and LV) is

Table 4.2   Welfare impact simulations with different measures, computation methods and scenarios

|  | S1 | S2 | S3 | S4 | S5 | S6 |
|---|---|---|---|---|---|---|
| *Price changes* | | | | | | |
| $dp_1$ | 0.1 | 0.5 | 5 | 0.1 | 0.5 | 2.5 |
| $dp_2$ | 0 | 0 | 0 | 0.05 | 0.5 | 5 |
| $dp_3$ | 0 | 0 | 0 | 0.025 | 0.5 | 10 |
| $dp_4$ | 0 | 0 | 0 | 0 | 0 | 0 |
| *Measures* | | | | | | |
| **LV** | −3.00 | −15.00 | −150.00 | −4.00 | −30.00 | −325.00 |
| **PV** | −2.73 | −10.00 | −25.00 | −3.69 | −20.00 | −47.94 |
| **CS True value** | −2.86 | −12.16 | −53.75 | −3.84 | −24.33 | −103.46 |
| CS Elasticity | −2.84 | −9.38 | 2100.00 | −3.82 | −18.75 | 11753.13 |
| CS_TAYLOR_2 | −2.85 | −11.25 | 225.00 | −3.83 | −22.50 | 893.75 |
| CS_TAYLOR_3 | −2.86 | −12.50 | −400.00 | −3.84 | −25.00 | −121.88 |
| **EV True value** | −2.82 | −11.45 | −41.58 | −3.77 | −21.59 | −64.46 |
| EV_TAYLOR_2 | −2.81 | −10.13 | 337.50 | −3.75 | −18.00 | 1421.88 |
| EV_TAYLOR_3 | −2.82 | −12.24 | −718.75 | −3.77 | −22.01 | −159.11 |
| EV Vartia | −2.80 | −11.16 | −37.21 | −3.75 | −21.29 | −60.46 |
| EV-Breslaw | −2.82 | −11.45 | −41.23 | −3.77 | −21.59 | −64.01 |
| EV-Euler | −2.80 | −11.15 | −35.60 | −3.75 | −21.19 | −55.49 |
| EV-RK4 | −2.82 | −11.45 | −41.58 | −3.77 | −21.74 | −66.11 |
| **CV True value** | −2.90 | −12.93 | −71.18 | −3.92 | −27.54 | −181.39 |
| CV_TAYLOR_2 | −2.89 | −12.38 | 112.50 | −3.91 | −27.00 | 365.63 |
| CV_TAYLOR_3 | −2.90 | −12.76 | −81.25 | −3.92 | −27.99 | −84.64 |
| CV Vartia | −2.92 | −13.31 | −85.45 | −3.93 | −28.02 | −214.54 |
| CV-Breslaw | −2.90 | −12.93 | −69.74 | −3.92 | −27.54 | −174.95 |
| CV-Euler | −2.92 | −13.29 | −84.04 | −3.93 | −28.02 | −207.57 |
| CV-RK4 | −2.90 | −12.93 | −71.18 | −3.91 | −27.31 | −170.65 |

Source: Author's calculations

5% for scenario 2 and 10% for scenario 5 with a price increase of 50% (one price or multiple prices).

• The difference between measures is extremely large and also nonsense for large price increases (above 100%, S3 and S6). Results show that the welfare effects can be larger than initial expenditure, which is a non-sense, and also varies enormously across measures and computation methods. For some methods, even the sign changes. As a general rule, linear approximations, as that of Taylor or CS elasticity, start to give odd results when the change in price exceeds the unity. For the Taylor approach, we can recall the two main sources of errors:

1. *The truncation error* which is related to the higher orders excluded from the estimations
2. *The convergence error* when the change is outside of the range of convergence of a specific approximated function

In the case of the Cobb–Douglas model (and for many other preference models), the Taylor approximation generates an infinite geometric series with a bounded range of convergence, as shown in Sect. 3.1.4. This explains the odd results that we obtain with the Taylor approximation where the price change exceeds unity.

- The one-step Taylor approximation requires higher orders when the price changes converge to the unity.
- The Breslaw and Smith (1995) approach is the most efficient and the closer to true values since it uses the numerical evaluation of the Slutsky matrix—together with the second-order Taylor approximation. Note how well it performs also for very large price increases.
- In general, the measurements that require some information related to the function form of preferences give more precise results, as is the case for Vartia, Breslaw, Euler and RK4 methods.
- The RK4 method shows a good performance, even if the price changes are relatively large.
- When the price changes are moderate (less than 10% or even until 20%), the practitioner can use any simple approximation method and the $LV$ is considered to be a good proxy of the $CV$.
- When the price change exceeds unity, the error attached to the linear approximation becomes very large and methods based on linear approximations are inadequate. We saw that the particular shape of the non-linear preferences function is not important and that a simple Cobb–Douglas function is sufficient.

We now construct a simple contour plot depicting the divergence (convergence) of estimations resulting from different methods using the two most relevant discriminatory factors: price change and expenditure share. As a measure of variation across methods, we use the difference between the upper (LV) and lower (PV) bounds of the measures normalized by initial expenditure ($m = 100$) and call this measure GAP. This provides a simple but accurate visual device that can be used by practitioners to take decisions on when to use simple LV estimations and when, instead, it is necessary to use more complex estimation procedures. Figure 4.10 shows the contour map for one price change (Panel a) and two price changes (Panel b). The different colored thresholds represent the GAP measure along 5% cut points. For example, if there is one price shock (Panel a) of 20% on a product that represents 10% of the consumption basket of a household, then the GAP is largely below 5% of income. It can be noted here that the higher is the expenditure share, the lower is the GAP. This is mainly explained by the low substitution effect (low compensated cross-elasticities) with the high expenditure share. It is natural that the GAP will depend on the expenditure share and will not exceed it. Panel b in Fig. 4.10 shows similar estimates when we consider two price changes such that $\alpha_2 = 0.2$ and $dp_2 = 0.5dp_1$.

Table 4.3 provides a numerical example of what we showed in Fig. 4.10 (Panel b). It is evident that the estimates of the GAP increase quickly as we move along rows from moderate price increases to large price increases. The GAP also increases as the share of expenditure on the product considered ($\alpha$) increases, but the pace of increase is much more modest. As it is clear by now, $\alpha$ and $\delta p$ are the two key parameters to watch when making a choice between $LV$ and more complex measures with $\delta p$ being the single most important factor.

### 4.1.2    Social Welfare

So far, the book has discussed differences across welfare estimation methods at the individual household level. When we stated the basic assumptions of this book, we also mentioned that we consider social welfare as the sum of individual welfare, which makes the formulation of all social welfare measures straightforward. Individual welfare effects due to price changes will be different across individuals whatever measure we use because initial consumption and the share of products in the consumption basket are usually different across individuals. Therefore, we should expect to have a distribution of individual welfare effects for any of the measures considered in this book.

In this section, we maintain the initial assumptions and we will not attempt to address issues of heterogeneity of the impact across individuals. However, working with a distribution of welfare changes, as opposed to individual welfare changes, opens the possibility of using statistical

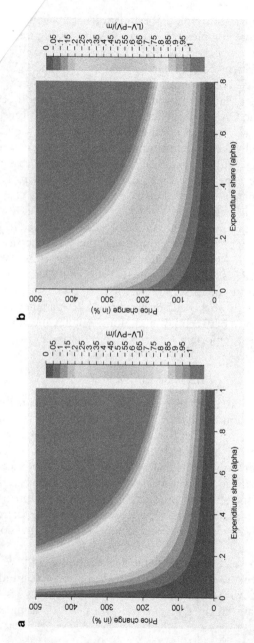

**Fig. 4.10** Contour map of the GAP estimations by price changes and expenditure shares. Panel **a**: One price change. Panel **b**: Two price changes. Source: Author's calculations

**Table 4.3** The normalized GAP estimations by price changes and expenditure shares

| $\alpha_1$ | The change in price $dp_1$ | | | | | | | | | |
|---|---|---|---|---|---|---|---|---|---|---|
| | 10% | 20% | 30% | 40% | 50% | 60% | 70% | 80% | 90% | 100% |
| 0 | 0.0000 | 0.0000 | 0.0000 | 0.0000 | 0.0000 | 0.0000 | 0.0000 | 0.0000 | 0.0000 | 0.0000 |
| 0.05 | −0.0011 | −0.0048 | −0.0106 | −0.0182 | −0.0273 | −0.0378 | −0.0495 | −0.0622 | −0.0758 | −0.0902 |
| 0.1 | −0.0015 | −0.0063 | −0.0139 | −0.0237 | −0.0354 | −0.0488 | −0.0636 | −0.0796 | −0.0967 | −0.1148 |
| 0.15 | −0.0019 | −0.0078 | −0.0171 | −0.0291 | −0.0435 | −0.0597 | −0.0777 | −0.0970 | −0.1177 | −0.1394 |
| 0.2 | −0.0023 | −0.0094 | −0.0204 | −0.0346 | −0.0515 | −0.0707 | −0.0917 | −0.1145 | −0.1386 | −0.1641 |
| 0.25 | −0.0026 | −0.0109 | −0.0236 | −0.0401 | −0.0596 | −0.0816 | −0.1058 | −0.1319 | −0.1596 | −0.1887 |
| 0.3 | −0.0030 | −0.0124 | −0.0269 | −0.0456 | −0.0676 | −0.0926 | −0.1199 | −0.1493 | −0.1805 | −0.2133 |
| 0.35 | −0.0034 | −0.0139 | −0.0302 | −0.0510 | −0.0757 | −0.1035 | −0.1340 | −0.1668 | −0.2015 | −0.2379 |
| 0.4 | −0.0037 | −0.0154 | −0.0334 | −0.0565 | −0.0837 | −0.1145 | −0.1481 | −0.1842 | −0.2225 | −0.2626 |
| 0.45 | −0.0041 | −0.0169 | −0.0367 | −0.0620 | −0.0918 | −0.1254 | −0.1622 | −0.2016 | −0.2434 | −0.2872 |
| 0.5 | −0.0045 | −0.0185 | −0.0399 | −0.0674 | −0.0999 | −0.1363 | −0.1763 | −0.2191 | −0.2644 | −0.3118 |
| 0.55 | −0.0049 | −0.0200 | −0.0432 | −0.0729 | −0.1079 | −0.1473 | −0.1903 | −0.2365 | −0.2853 | −0.3364 |
| 0.6 | −0.0052 | −0.0215 | −0.0465 | −0.0784 | −0.1160 | −0.1582 | −0.2044 | −0.2539 | −0.3063 | −0.3611 |
| 0.65 | −0.0056 | −0.0230 | −0.0497 | −0.0839 | −0.1240 | −0.1692 | −0.2185 | −0.2714 | −0.3272 | −0.3857 |
| 0.70 | −0.0060 | −0.0245 | −0.0530 | −0.0893 | −0.1321 | −0.1801 | −0.2326 | −0.2888 | −0.3482 | −0.4103 |
| 0.75 | −0.0063 | −0.0260 | −0.0562 | −0.0948 | −0.1401 | −0.1911 | −0.2467 | −0.3062 | −0.3691 | −0.4349 |
| 0.8 | −0.0067 | −0.0276 | −0.0595 | −0.1003 | −0.1482 | −0.2020 | −0.2608 | −0.3237 | −0.3901 | −0.4596 |
| 0.85 | −0.0071 | −0.0291 | −0.0628 | −0.1057 | −0.1563 | −0.2130 | −0.2749 | −0.3411 | −0.4111 | −0.4842 |
| 0.9 | −0.0075 | −0.0306 | −0.0660 | −0.1112 | −0.1643 | −0.2239 | −0.2889 | −0.3585 | −0.4320 | −0.5088 |
| 0.95 | −0.0078 | −0.0321 | −0.0693 | −0.1167 | −0.1724 | −0.2349 | −0.3030 | −0.3760 | −0.4530 | −0.5334 |
| 1 | −0.0082 | −0.0336 | −0.0725 | −0.1222 | −0.1804 | −0.2458 | −0.3171 | −0.3934 | −0.4739 | −0.5581 |

Source: Author's calculations

inference for testing differences across social welfare distributions. We can also test statistical differences across measures for quantiles rather than for the entire distribution, and we can start discussing how different welfare estimation methods differ for different parts of the welfare distribution. This is important because, as we stated in the introduction, this book is mainly concerned about poor people and poor countries. Moreover, by shifting the analysis to the distribution of welfare, we can also borrow from welfare economics and the very rich literature on distributional analysis and use instruments such as stochastic dominance or pro-poor curves to refine our assessment of the difference between welfare estimation measures. This is what this section is about. We will start by introducing a possible strategy to estimate standard errors at the social and quantile levels, and we will finish by introducing pro-poor curves for comparing welfare estimation methods.

**Statistical Inference (Society)**
The questions we address are the following: Are the differences between means of welfare estimation methods statistically significant? And can these statistical tests help us to discriminate between welfare estimation methods? Most analysts work with sample surveys, and welfare estimates such as $LV$ or $CS$ will contain a sampling error. For each sampled household $i$, one can estimate the net impact on well-being: $\Delta v_i = f(\Delta p_1, \ldots, \Delta p_k; \Delta m = tr_i)$ where $tr_i$ refers simply to the transfer to the individual $i$. Since the required information to assess $v_i$ comes only from the sampled households $i$, the variable $\Delta v$ will be $i.i.d.$ In general, the sample size of national household surveys is large, and, based on asymptotic theory and the case of large sample size, the distribution of any estimator will converge to the normal distribution. We need, therefore, to start by finding a proper approach to the estimation of the standard error of the difference between means of welfare estimation methods.

Suppose that we want to estimate the mean difference between $LV$ and $PV$, the upper and lower bounds of our welfare estimation methods. Let $\Delta_{PV,LV}$ denote the estimator of the mean difference, $N$ the simple size and

$I$ the number of goods so that:

$$\Delta_{PV,LV} = \mu_{PV} - \mu_{LV} \tag{4.3}$$

$$= \frac{1}{N} \sum_{j=1}^{N} \sum_{i=1}^{I} \left( -x_{j,i}^{b} dp_i \right) - \left( -x_{j,i}^{a} dp_i \right) \tag{4.4}$$

$$= \sum_{i=1}^{I} dp_i (\mu_{x_i^a} - \mu_{x_i^b}) \tag{4.5}$$

where $\mu_x$ denotes the average of $x$. For the case of Cobb–Douglas preferences, we have that $x_i^b = x_i^a/(1 + dp_i)$ where the initial price is assumed to be equal to 1. In this case, for multiple price changes, we have:

$$\Delta_{PV,LV} = \sum_{i=1}^{I} \left( \mu_{x_i^a} - \mu_{x_i^a} \frac{1}{(1+dp)} \right) dp_i \tag{4.6}$$

$$= \sum_{i=1}^{I} \frac{dp_i^2}{1+dp_i} \mu_{x_i^a}. \tag{4.7}$$

It follows that the standard error of the mean difference for a single price change can be estimated as:

$$\sigma_{\Delta_{PV,LV}} = \frac{dp_1^2}{1+dp_1} \sigma_{\mu_{x_1^a}} \tag{4.8}$$

Similarly, if we wish to estimate the standard error of the mean difference between $CS$ with Cobb–Douglas preferences and $LV$, we can derive the estimation of the standard error as follows:

$$\sigma_{\Delta_{CS,LV}} = (dp_1 - \log(1 + dp_1)) \, \sigma_{\mu_{x_1^a}} \tag{4.9}$$

Since the estimator of $\Delta_{CS,LV}$ uses two basic estimators ($\mu_{CS}$ and $\mu_{LV}$), the delta method can be used to estimate the standard error (see Rao (1973)).

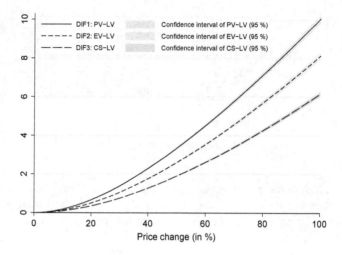

**Fig. 4.11** The difference between welfare measurements. Source: Author's calculations

*Single Price Change* We are now in a position to test statistically the mean difference between welfare estimation methods at the societal level. To illustrate these tests, we use data from the 1987/88 *Nationwide Food Consumption Survey*, which is conducted by the United States Department of Agriculture. We simulate price increases between 0 and 100% of *meats* and test mean differences between $PV$, $EV$, $CS$ and $LV$ in turn using 95% confidence intervals. As shown in Fig. 4.11, differences across welfare estimation methods are visible starting from price increases in between 10% and 20%, while confidence intervals remain rather narrow until price increases of 100%. For example, with a price increase of 85%, the mean difference between $PV$ and $LV$ is around 8 percentage points, but the confidence interval around that difference is a fraction of a percentage point at the 95% confidence level. In other words, confidence intervals do not really put into question the remarkable difference across welfare estimation methods already very evident beyond price increases of 10–20%.

*Multiple Price Changes* Of course, price changes may be more complex than one simple price increase and may include increases as well as decreases in prices. Using the same set of data, assume that the price reform concerns two goods with a decrease of 45% in the price of *fruits and vegetables* and an

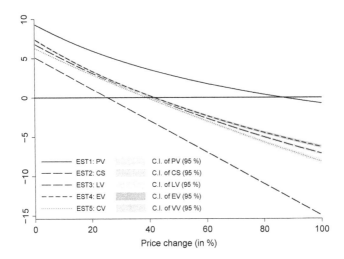

**Fig. 4.12**  The welfare measurements and the sampling errors. Source: Author's calculations

increase between 0% and 100% in the price of *meats*. As shown in Fig. 4.12, two main lessons can be drawn. First, the judgment on the impact of the price reform on welfare can depend on the selected measure of welfare change. For instance, for an increase of 60% in the price of *meats*, only the *PV* measurement indicates an improvement in welfare. The second lesson concerns the gray area for which one cannot make any judgment about the nature of the impact. For instance, for the range [83%, 90%] of increase in the price of *meats*, the impact measured by *PV* is not significantly different from 0. In essence, statistical inference can help in determining whether the impact of one welfare measure is significantly different from zero, but beyond price increases of 10–20% confidence intervals are too narrow to overlap across measures. Hence, all the empirical results reported for individual welfare effects and related to differences between welfare measures largely apply to mean social welfare.

### Statistical Inference (Quantiles)
Quantiles are sub-sets of samples (populations) and, by definition, smaller sets than samples (populations), which makes statistical inference more complex. In this section, we provide one possible approach to estimate the

standard error of the mean difference between welfare estimation methods by quantile.

Let $\tau_1$ and $\tau_2$ be two successive percentiles defining a given population group (for instance, the second quintile is the one with incomes $y > Q(\tau_1 = 0.2)$ and $y \leq Q(\tau_2 = 0.4)$ and $Q(\tau)$ is the quantile at percentile $\tau$. The average impact of a price reform on the welfare of group $g(\tau_1, \tau_2)$ is defined as follows:

$$\hat{\mu}(\tau_1, \tau_2) = \frac{N^{-1} \sum \omega_i y_i I[y_i \leq \hat{Q}(\tau_2)] - N^{-1} \sum \omega_i y_i I[y_i \leq \hat{Q}(\tau_1)]}{N^{-1} \sum \omega_i I[y_i \leq \hat{Q}(\tau_2)] - N^{-1} \sum \omega_i I[y_i \leq \hat{Q}(\tau_1)]}$$

$$= \frac{\hat{\alpha}_2 - \hat{\alpha}_1}{\hat{\beta}_2 - \hat{\beta}_1} \qquad (4.10)$$

where $I[true] = 1$ and zero otherwise, $\omega_i$ is the final weight (for instance, the product of sampling weights times household size).

This estimator is a function of four basic estimators ($\alpha_*$, and $\beta_*$). For simplicity, let $\hat{\alpha}_1 = N^{-1} \sum a_i$ and $a_i = \omega_i y_i I[y_i < \hat{Q}(\tau_1)]$. As we can observe, the elements of the new generated variable $(a)$ are not i.i.d, since each element $(a_i)$ is based on another estimate $(\hat{Q}(\tau_1))$ and this implicit variability will affect the variance of our basic estimator.

One way to estimate accurately the standard error is by correcting for this implicit variability using the Rao (1973) approach. In what follows, we define the variance of the estimators $\alpha_1$ and $\beta_1$ (those of $\alpha_2$ and that of $\beta_2$ are quite similar) as:

$$Var(\hat{\alpha}_1) = N^{-1} STD \left( \omega \left( y I[y \leq \hat{Q}(\tau_1)] - F(\hat{Q}(\tau_1)) \right) \right.$$
$$\left. \times \left( I[\hat{Q}(\tau_1) \leq y] - \tau_1 \right) / f(\hat{Q}(\tau_1)) \right) \qquad (4.11)$$

$$Var(\hat{\beta}_1) = N^{-1} STD \left( \omega \left( I[y \leq \hat{Q}(\tau_1)] - F(\hat{Q}(\tau_1)) \right) \right.$$
$$\left. \times \left( I[\hat{Q}(\tau_1) \leq y] - \tau_1 \right) \right) \qquad (4.12)$$

where $STD(V)$ is the standard deviation of the variable $V$, and $f(.)$ and $F(.)$ denote respectively the density function and its cumulative.

Is the estimated standard error of $\mu(\tau_1, \tau_2)$ significantly different from that when we omit to take into account the implicit variability, that is,

**Table 4.4**  Estimated statistics for the fourth quintile

| Estimator | Estimated value |
| --- | --- |
| Estimated average | 8503.57 |
| STE: Analytical approach (without considering the implicit variability) | 20.26 |
| STE: Analytical approach | 67.37 |
| STE: Bootstrap (number of replications = 400) | 68.57 |

Source: Author's calculations

when we assume that $Var(\hat{\alpha}_1) = N^{-1} STD\left(yI[y \leq \hat{Q}(\tau_1)]\right)$? To answer this question and to validate the proposed method for the estimation of the STE, we use a sample of 6000 randomly generated observations.[3] Table 4.4 shows the estimates for the fourth quintile. The estimated STE with the bootstrap approach is close to that estimated with the proposed analytical approach. Instead, omitting the correction for the implicit variability will give a wrong estimate of the STE.

## Pro-poor Curves and Stochastic Dominance

Having a method for statistical inference at the quantile level, we can now use it to draw and compare pro-poor price reform curves. There are different interpretations of what pro-poor means, and this has been the object of debate in the welfare economics literature with some arguing that pro-poor means that the poor outperform the non-poor and other arguing that a pro-poor reform is one that simply makes the poor better off, whether they outperform the non-poor or not (Ravallion and Chen 2003; Kakwani and Pernia 2000; Son 2004; Duclos 2009). Irrespective of these different views, assessing pro-poorness implies comparing welfare impacts across quantiles, and this can be done with what is known as pro-poor curves. One can then use a standard stochastic dominance approach to determine whether one distribution dominates another or not. In our case, each pro-poor curve can be constructed using the pre and post price reform for each welfare estimation method. We can then check for the pro-poorness of the impact with the different welfare measurements and by using stochastic dominance theory. Remember that a pro-poor curve for a welfare estimation method is first-order welfare dominant if

---

[3] We used the Stata command *gen imp_wel = _n\*(3+0.05\*uniform())*.

and only if:

$$\lambda_1(\tau) = \frac{Q^b(\tau) - Q^a(\tau)}{Q^a(\tau)} - \varrho > 0 \qquad \forall \tau \in [0, \tau^*] \qquad (4.13)$$

where $\varrho$ is simply the average impact of the price reform and $\tau^*$ is a given critical percentile. The critical value marks the limit of the test, which is simply the highest possible proportion of poor. Recall here that, among the Social Welfare Functions (SWFs) that obey to the first-order dominance constraint, some do not attribute more importance to the poor. For unequivocal comparisons, we need a second-order dominance test as follows:

$$\lambda_2(\tau) = \frac{C^b(\tau) - C^a(\tau)}{C^a(\tau)} - \varrho > 0 \qquad \forall \tau \in [0, \tau^*] \qquad (4.14)$$

where $C(p)$ is simply the generalized Lorenz curve (see, for instance, Son (2004)). The estimator of the variance of the quantile $Q(\tau)$ and the generalized Lorenz curve can be defined as follows:

$$\hat{Var}((Q(\tau))) = N^{-1} \sum \left( I[y_i \le \hat{Q}(\tau)] - \tau \right) / f(\hat{Q}(\tau)) \qquad (4.15)$$

$$\hat{Var}((C(\tau))) = N^{-1} \sum \left( \tau Q(\tau) + (y_i - Q(\tau)) I[y_i \le \hat{Q}(\tau)] \right) \qquad (4.16)$$

To illustrate these instruments, we use again data from the 1987/88 *Nationwide Food Consumption Survey*. Assume that the price reform include an increase of 20% in the price of *meats* and a reduction of 20% in the price of *fruits and vegetables*. Figures 4.13 and 4.14 show first- and second-order dominance of the pro-poor curves constructed with the *LV* and *CS* methods, the latter with Cobb–Douglas preferences. As one can observe, the simulated price reform is pro-poor even if the change in prices does not affect government revenues significantly (the curve averages around zero). It can also be noted that the *LV* and *CS* curves largely overlap indicating that there is little difference between measures for this particular price reform. In this case, the use of *LV* would be appropriate and also simplify computation.

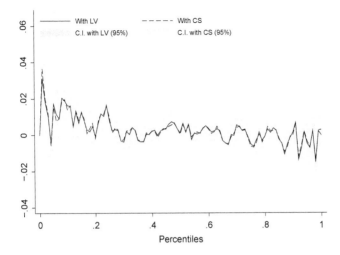

**Fig. 4.13**  First-order pro-poor price reform curve (small price changes). Source: Author's calculations

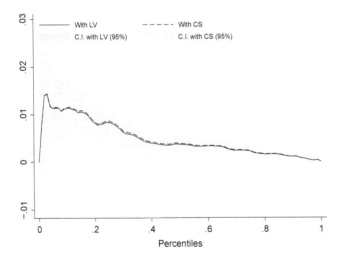

**Fig. 4.14**  Second-order pro-poor price reform curve (small price changes). Source: Author's calculations

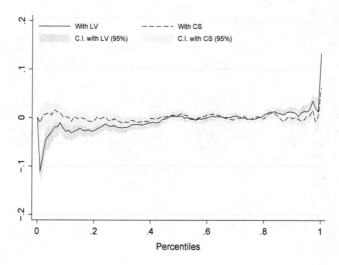

**Fig. 4.15** First-order pro-poor price reform curve (large price changes). Source: Author's calculations

As we have learned by now, the differences across measures diverge as prices increase. We therefore repeat the exercise with a large price increase, an increase in the price of meats of 100%. Figures 4.15 and 4.16 show that the $LV$ and $CS$ measures provide very different results and the difference is greater for lower quantiles (the poor). The reason for the difference between the $LV$ and $CS$ measures is the fact that the share of expenditure represented by the product affected by price changes varies across the welfare distribution and this share is used by the CS method (alpha in the Cobb–Douglas formula) but not by the $LV$ method. This is one more reason to be very weary of the differences across measures. As prices increase, the differences across measures increase, they are significant and they can be larger for lower parts of the distributions. This makes estimates of the welfare effects on poverty even more complex than estimates for an entire society.

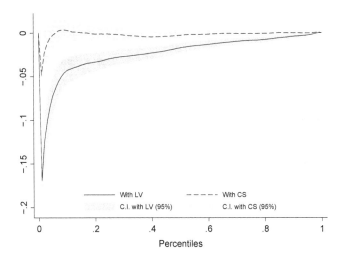

**Fig. 4.16** Second-order pro-poor price reform curve (large price changes). Source: Author's calculations

## REFERENCES

BANKS, J., R. BLUNDELL, AND A. LEWBEL (1996): "Tax Reform and Welfare Measurement: Do We Need Demand System Estimation?" *Economic Journal*, 106, 1227–41.

—— (1997): "Quadratic Engel Curves And Consumer Demand," *The Review of Economics and Statistics*, 79, 527–539.

BRESLAW, J. A. AND J. B. SMITH (1995): "A Simple and Efficient Method for Estimating the Magnitude and Precision of Welfare Changes," *Journal of Applied Econometrics*, 10, 313–27.

DEATON, A. AND J. MUELLBAUER (1980): "An Almost Ideal Demand System," *American Economic Review*, 70, 312–336.

DUCLOS, J.-Y. (2009): "What is Pro-Poor?" *Social Choice and Welfare*, 32, 37–58.

HICKS, J. R. (1942): "Consumers' Surplus and Index-Numbers," *The Review of Economic Studies*, 9, 126–137.

KAKWANI, N. AND E. PERNIA (2000): "What is Pro Poor Growth?" *Asian Development Review*, 18, 1–16.

LEWBEL, A. AND K. PENDAKUR (2009): "Tricks with Hicks: The EASI Demand System," *American Economic Review*, 99, 827–63.

RAMSKOV, J. AND J. MUNKSGAARD (2001): "Elasticities a Theoretical Introduction," Tech. rep., Balmorel Project: http://balmorel.com/doc/b-elasttheory0201.pdf.

RAO, R. (1973): *Linear Statistical Inference and Its Applications*, New York: John Wiley and Sons Inc.

RAVALLION, M. AND S. CHEN (2003): "Measuring Pro-poor Growth," *Economics Letters*, 78, 93–99.

SON, H. (2004): "A note on pro-poor growth," *Economics Letters*, 82, 307–314.

# CHAPTER 5

# Conclusion

The book studied the theoretical and empirical properties of the five most popular measures used in economics to capture welfare changes when prices change. We adopted a number of standard assumptions including monotonic and strictly convex utility functions; single-valued and continuously differentiable demand functions; complete, reflexive and transitive preferences; constant marginal utility of income; utility maximizing consumers; and normal goods. The theoretical part provided definitions, geometrical illustration and various computation options for all measures and led to the following conclusions:

- The welfare effects is bounded between $LV = (-)x^a dp$ and $PV = (-)x^b dp$.
- $LV < CV < CS < EV < PV$ if $dp \neq 0$ (if the demand schedules are not perfectly elastic or inelastic).
- $LV \neq CV \neq CS \neq EV \neq PV$ if $dp \neq 0$ (if the demand schedules are not perfectly elastic or inelastic).
- $LV = CV = CS = EV = PV$ with a perfectly elastic or inelastic Marshallian demand schedule.
- With a price change in only one product, marginal utility of money constant and a quadratic approximation, $CV$, $CS$ and $EV$ can be approximated to the same measure.
- $CV$, $CS$, $EV$ and $PV$ can all be expressed as functions of $LV$ and the income and substitution effects.

© The Author(s) 2019                                                          75
A. Araar, P. Verme, *Prices and Welfare*,
https://doi.org/10.1007/978-3-030-17423-1_5

- The first-order and higher-order Taylor's approximations can always be split into an income and a substitution effect.
- For small price changes, the substitution effect of the first-order Taylor's approximation can be approximated to zero.
- For small price changes and with a first-order Taylor's approximation, $CS$, $CV$ and $EV$ can be approximated to the same measure.
- With a marginal income change, changes in consumed goods converge to their expenditure shares.
- When the expenditure share is small, the corrected first Taylor approximation term is a good proxy of the income effect, whereas the rest is a good proxy of the substitution effect.
- With small price changes, the Taylor approximation converges to the $CS$ measure.

The empirical part tested the sensitivity of the welfare measure to changes in various parameters including price shocks, demand functions, consumption bundles (shares of products in total consumption) and elasticities. This exercise provided broad indications that can be used by practitioners to make choices between measures. In particular:

- With a small or moderate price change, "LV" (the *marginal approach*) becomes the appropriate measure to assess the change in welfare.
- Price changes can be considered "small" in all cases if they are below 10%.
- Differences between the five measures considered are very sensitive to the expenditure share of products.
- If the expenditure share on the product that is affected by the price change is small, then price changes of up to 50% can be considered small.
- The contour plot provided by the book can be used as a device to decide when welfare outcomes between measures are too large to use the simplest of the measures considered ($LV$).
- Differences between the five measures considered are not particularly sensitive to the various demand functions considered (CD, QUAIDS, AIDS, EASI and LES).
- With changes in prices of multiple products, the welfare effect is reduced and the bounds at which welfare measure grow apart can be relaxed.

- For large price variations, and with knowledge of the free market point elasticity, one can use Eq. 3.20 to avoid making full assumptions about demand schedules. This stratagem is fairly close to using Cobb–Douglas preferences up to price variations of about 100 percent and is very parsimonious in terms of information required.
- Confidence intervals (95%) for the welfare measures considered do not seem to alter the conclusions above.
- When welfare measures provide very different results, the choice of the measure is ultimately a normative choice.
- In the absence of any normative argument in favor of one particular measure, the sensible choice is $CS$ for the simple reason that this measure is always the median measure.
- In the absence of any normative argument in favor of one demand function, the sensible choice is the Cobb–Douglas function because of its simplicity and nice properties in relation to utility curves.

Finally, it is evident that if one considers the price shock of only one product and this product is a small share of household expenditure, the measure of choice is invariably $LV$. But in the real world, it is not very common to model situations when price increases and expenditure shares are both small, whether we consider subsidies, taxes or changes in inflation. For example, it is not uncommon in developing countries to have subsidies that are several folds the subsidized price so that the price increase necessary to remove subsidies is measured in the hundreds of percentage points. Similarly, imposing sales taxes on a particular product can increase prices by 20–30%, and this is not uncommon in developing countries where a typical sales tax is around 20%. In these cases, the expenditure share of products may be small but the price increases are large. In other cases, such as a longitudinal or spatial inflation adjustments, the price adjustment may be relatively small but the share of expenditure concerned by the inflation adjustment is very large (the whole products' basket). And it is not atypical for developing countries to experience periods of hyperinflation. Hence, practitioners rarely find situations where the price increase considered and the expenditure share of the products considered are both small. It is also rare for practitioners working on developing countries to be able to measure the Marshallian demand schedule. In the case of subsidies, prices are fixed by definition and surveys cannot provide the price variations necessary to estimate demand schedules. In the case of taxes, few developing countries have proper tax systems in place and fewer have populations that comply to the tax systems, and this makes estimations of tax elasticities impossible. This book has provided some initial guidelines on what to do under different circumstances and degree of information.

# APPENDICES

## A.1   DEMAND SYSTEMS

### A.1.1   Linear Demand (LD)

$$q = a - bp \tag{A.1}$$

$$p = \frac{a}{b} - \frac{1}{b}q \tag{A.2}$$

$$\eta = -b\frac{p}{q} \tag{A.3}$$

### A.1.2   Log Linear Demand (LLD)

$$q = e^a p^- b \tag{A.4}$$

$$ln(q) = a - ln(p)b \tag{A.5}$$

$$p = (e^{-a}q)^{-\frac{1}{b}} \tag{A.6}$$

$$\eta = \frac{\partial ln(q)}{\partial ln(p)} = -b \tag{A.7}$$

© The Author(s) 2019
A. Araar, P. Verme, *Prices and Welfare*,
https://doi.org/10.1007/978-3-030-17423-1

### A.1.3   The Linear Expenditure System (LES)

The LES model assumes that expenditures depend linearly on income and prices. The LES specification derives from the maximization of a linear Stone–Geary utility function such that:

$$Max\, U = \sum_{k=1}^{K} \beta_k \ln (x_k - \gamma_k);\qquad\text{(A.8)}$$

subject to the budget constraint and the Engel aggregation condition:

$$m = \sum_{k=1}^{K} p_k x_k, \text{ and } \sum_{k=1}^{K} \beta_k = 1 \qquad\text{(A.9)}$$

The econometric model of the demand function of household $h$ for commodity $k$:

$$x_k = \gamma_k + \frac{\beta_k}{p_k}\left(m - \sum_{k=1}^{K} p_k \gamma_k\right). \qquad\text{(A.10)}$$

There are $(2K - 1)$ parameters ( $\beta_s$ and $\gamma_s$ to be estimated). Expenditure on a given good is a linear function in income and prices. However, the expenditure system is not linear in parameters. Note that the non-homotheticity introduced by the subsistence quantities ($\gamma_k$) allows the LES to exhibit non-unitary expenditure elasticities. The model can be estimated through maximum likelihood using the Stata **nlsur** command. (This fits a system of non-linear equations by feasible generalized non-linear least squares.) The Marshallian price elasticities are:

$$\varepsilon_{k,k} = \frac{\gamma_k (1 - \beta_k)}{x_k} - 1 \text{ and } \varepsilon_{k,l} = -\beta_k \frac{p_l \gamma_l}{p_k \bar{x}} \qquad\text{(A.11)}$$

The compensated price elasticities are:

$$\eta_{k,k} = (\beta_k - 1)\left(1 - \frac{\gamma_k}{x_k}\right) \text{ and } \eta_{k,h} = -\frac{\beta_k p_h}{p_k x_k}(x_k - \gamma_h) \qquad\text{(A.12)}$$

The income elasticity is:

$$\eta_k = \frac{\beta_k m}{p_k x_k} - 1. \tag{A.13}$$

Note that the indirect utility of the LES model takes the following form:

$$V(m, p) = \frac{m - \sum_{k=1}^{K} p_k \gamma_k}{\prod_{k=1}^{K} p_k^{\beta_k}} \tag{A.14}$$

Let $\varsigma_k = \frac{p_k}{p_k + dp_k}$. It can be shown that:

$$EV_{LES} = m \left( \prod_{k=1}^{K} \varsigma^{\beta_k} - 1 \right) + \sum_{k=1}^{K} p_k \gamma_k - \prod_{k=1}^{K} \varsigma^{\beta_k} \left( \sum_{k=1}^{K} (p_k + dp_k)\gamma_k \right) \tag{A.15}$$

Remember that the equivalent variation with the CD model can be written as follows:

$$EV_{CD} = m \left( \prod_{k=1}^{K} \varsigma^{\alpha_k} - 1 \right) \tag{A.16}$$

With moderate estimates of $\gamma_k$, $\beta_k$ converges to $\alpha_k$, that is, the expenditure share. Based on this, and by comparing the two impacts, we find that:

$$\theta(P, m) = \frac{EV_{LES}}{EV_{CD}} = 1 + \frac{\sum_{k=1}^{K} p_k \gamma_k - \prod_{k=1}^{K} \varsigma^{\beta_k} \left( \sum_{k=1}^{K} (p_k + dp_k)\gamma_k \right)}{m \left( \prod_{k=1}^{K} \varsigma^{\beta_k} - 1 \right)} \tag{A.17}$$

Let $\tau = \sum_{k=1}^{K} p_k \gamma_k$ denote the expenditures on the initial dotations and $d\tau = \sum_{k=1}^{K} dp_k \gamma_k$. We can simplify again and find:

$$\theta(P, m) = 1 - \frac{\tau}{m} + \frac{d\tau}{m} \frac{\prod_{k=1}^{K} \varsigma^{\beta_k}}{1 - \prod_{k=1}^{K} \varsigma^{\beta_k}} \tag{A.18}$$

With a single price change we find that:

$$\theta(P, m) = 1 - \frac{\tau}{m} + \frac{d\tau}{m} \frac{\varsigma^{\beta_k}}{1 - \varsigma^{\beta_k}} \tag{A.19}$$

Even if $\theta(P, m)$ is divergent when $p_k \to \infty$, it follows that with rational large price changes, the $EV_{CD}$ is a good proxy of $EV_{LES}$. Let $m = 100$, $\beta_k = 0.2$, $\gamma_k = 2$, $\tau = 10$ and $p_k = 1 \; \forall k$. With a price change of 500%, we find that *theta* $\approx 1.178$. In essence, we can say that, with reasonable large price variations, it is expected that EV estimated with the CD model can be a good proxy of EV with the LES model.

### A.1.4   The Almost Ideal Demand System (AIDS)

To present the AIDS model, we start by defining the PIGLOG model. This model can be represented via an expenditure function $c(\mathbf{P}, U)$ that defines the minimum level of expenditure to reach a predetermined level of utility given prevailing prices:

$$\log(c(p, U)) = (1 - U) \log(a(p)) + U \log(b(p)) \tag{A.20}$$

where $U$ is the utility located between 0, the level of subsistence, and 1, the level of beatitude. The function $a(p)$ is found through the TRANSLOG form:

$$\log(a(p)) = \alpha_0 + \sum_{i=1}^{K} \alpha_i \log(p_i) + \sum_{i=1}^{K} \sum_{j=1}^{K} \gamma_{i,j}^* \log(p_i) \log(p_j) \tag{A.21}$$

The component $b(p)$ is defined as:

$$\log(b(p)) = \log(a(p)) + \beta_0 \prod_{i=1}^{K} p_i^{\beta_i} \tag{A.22}$$

Thus, we find that:

$$\log(c(p,u)) = \alpha_0 + \sum_{i=1}^{K} \alpha_i \log(p_i) + \sum_{i=1}^{K} \sum_{j=1}^{K} \gamma_{i,j}^* \log(p_i) \log(p_j)$$

$$+ u\beta_0 \prod_{i=1}^{K} p_i{}^{\beta_i} \tag{A.23}$$

Using Shephard's lemma $(\partial c(p,u)/\partial p_k = x_k)$ , the expenditure share on good $i$ becomes:

$$w_i = \alpha_i + \sum_{i=1}^{K} \sum_{j=1}^{K} \gamma_{i,j} \log(p_j) + \beta_i u \beta_0 \prod_{i=1}^{K} p_i{}^{\beta_i} \tag{A.24}$$

and

$$\gamma_{i,j} = \frac{1}{2} \left( \gamma_{i,j}^* + \gamma_{j,i}^* \right) \tag{A.25}$$

Expenditure shares also simplify as:

$$w_i = \alpha_i + \sum_{j=1}^{K} \gamma_{i,j} \log(p_j) + \beta_i \log(m/a(p)) \tag{A.26}$$

where $a(p)$ can be perceived as a price index equaling:

$$\log(a(p)) = \alpha_0 + \sum_{i=1}^{K} \alpha_i \log(p_i) + \sum_{i=1}^{K} \sum_{j=1}^{K} \gamma_{i,j}^* \log(p_i) \log(p_j) \tag{A.27}$$

The additional conditions of the model are:

$I: \sum_{i=1}^{K} \alpha_k = 1$        Sum of expenditures shares is 1

$II: \sum_{i=1}^{K} \gamma_{i,j} = 0 \,\forall j$ and $\sum_{i=1}^{K} \beta_i = 0$    Homogeneity of degree 0 of demand functions

$III: \gamma_{i,j} = \gamma_{j,i}$        Symmetry of the Slutsky matrix

$$\tag{A.28}$$

The indirect utility function is defined as follows:

$$Ln(V) = \left[ \frac{\ln(m) - \ln(a(p))}{b(p)} \right] \tag{A.29}$$

### A.1.5   The Quadratic Almost Ideal Demand System (QUAIDS)

Banks et al. (1997) have proposed the Quadratic Almost Ideal Demand System (QUAIDS) model that adds the quadratic logarithmic income term to the AIDS specification of Deaton and Muellbauer (1980). This was proposed in order to take into account the potential quadratic form of the Engel curve behavior for some durable and luxury goods. The specification is as follows:

$$w_i = \alpha_i + \sum_{j=1}^{K} \gamma_{i,j} \log(p_j) + \beta_i \log(m/a(p)) + \frac{\lambda_i}{b(p)} \log(m/a(p))^2 \tag{A.30}$$

The price index is given by:

$$\log(a(p)) = \alpha_0 + \sum_{i=1}^{K} \alpha_i \log(p_i) + \sum_{i=1}^{K} \sum_{j=1}^{K} \gamma_{i,j}^* \log(p_i) \log(p_j) \tag{A.31}$$

The price aggregator is given by:

$$b(p) = \prod_{i=1}^{K} p_i^{\beta_i} \tag{A.32}$$

The set of constraints to obey to the usual Marshallian properties are:

$$I: \sum_{i=1}^{K} \alpha_k = 1 \qquad \text{Sum of expenditures shares is 1}$$

$$II: \sum_{i=1}^{K} \gamma_{i,j} = 0 \; \forall j \text{ and } \sum_{i=1}^{K} \beta_i = 0 \qquad \text{Homogeneity of degree 0 of demand functions}$$

$$III: \gamma_{i,j} = \gamma_{j,i} \qquad \text{Symmetry of the Slutsky matrix}$$

$$\tag{A.33}$$

The income and demand elasticities are defined as follows:

$$I : \quad e_i = \mu_i/w_i - 1 \qquad \text{Income elasticity}$$
$$II : \quad e_{i,j}^{nc} = \mu_{i,j}/w_i - \delta_{i,j} \quad \text{Non compensated elasticity} \qquad (A.34)$$
$$III : e_{i,j}^{c} = \mu_{i,j}/w_i - e_i w_i \text{ Compensated elasticity}$$

where

$$\mu_i = \tfrac{\partial w_i}{\partial \log(m)} = \beta_i + 2\lambda_i \log\left(\tfrac{m}{a(p)}\right)$$

$$\mu_{i,j} = \tfrac{\partial w_i}{\partial \log(p_j)} = \gamma_{i,j} + \mu_i \left(\alpha_j + \sum_{k=1}^{K} \gamma_{k,j} \log(p_k)\right) - \tfrac{\lambda_i \beta_j}{b(p)} \left\{\log\left(\tfrac{m}{a(p)}\right)\right\}^2$$
$$(A.35)$$

The indirect utility function is defined as follows:

$$Ln(V) = \left[\left[\tfrac{\ln(m) - \ln(a(p))}{b(p)}\right]^{-1} + \lambda(p)\right]^{-1} \qquad (A.36)$$

and

$$\lambda(p) = \sum_{i=1}^{K} \lambda_i \log(p_i) \qquad (A.37)$$

### A.1.6    Exact Affine Stone Index (EASI)

To deal with the empirical non-linear form of the Engel curve and to propose a more flexible model, Lewbel and Pendakur (2009) use the Shephard's lemma to approximate real income. This linear approximation implies the use of the Stone price index (SPI), as in the case of the Linear Approximate Almost Ideal Demand System (LA/AIDS). Even with this restriction, among the advantages of the EASI model is the possibility of using a higher order of the polynomial real income, which enables to better fit the Engel function. Formally, the approximated EASI model can be defined through the implicit Marshallian budget share as follows:

$$w_i = \sum_{r=1}^{o} b_r \tilde{y}^r + \sum_{j=1}^{K} a_k \log(p_k) + \sum_{k=1}^{K} b_k \log(p_k) \tilde{y} + \tilde{\epsilon}$$

$$= \sum_{r=1}^{o} b_r \tilde{y}^r + \mathbf{Ap} + \mathbf{Bp}\tilde{y} + \tilde{\epsilon} \tag{A.38}$$

where $\tilde{y}$ denotes the log of the approximated real income: $y \approx \tilde{y} = \log(m) - \sum_{k=1}^{K} w_k \log(p_k)$.

The parameter $o$ is the polynomial order of the real income, and the parameter $\tilde{\epsilon}$ is simply the error term of the estimation. For simplicity and compared to the Lewbel and Pendakur (2009) presentation of the model, we omit the household characteristics determinants. Based on the Shephard's lemma and the cost function, Lewbel and Pendakur (2009) show that the exact real income is equal to:

$$y = \frac{m - \mathbf{p'w} + \mathbf{p'Ap}}{1 - 0.5 * \mathbf{p'Bp}} \tag{A.39}$$

Thus, the exact EASI model can be defined as follows:

$$w_i = \sum_{r=1}^{o} b_r \left( \frac{m - \mathbf{p'w} + \mathbf{p'Ap}}{1 - 0.5 * \mathbf{p'Bp}} \right)^r + \mathbf{Ap} + \mathbf{Bp} \left( \frac{m - \mathbf{p'w} + \mathbf{p'Ap}}{1 - 0.5 * \mathbf{p'Bp}} \right) + \epsilon \tag{A.40}$$

As was the case for the AIDS or the QUAIDS models, additional conditions are imposed:

$$I : \sum_{i=1}^{K} a_{i,j} = 0 \; \forall j \text{ and } \sum_{i=1}^{K} b_i = 0 \quad \text{Homogeneity of degree 0 of demand functions}$$

$$II : a_{i,j} = a_{j,i} \quad \text{Symmetry of the Slutsky matrix} \tag{A.41}$$

Among the recommended econometric methods to estimate the model is the non-linear three-stage least squares (3SLS). Let $\mathbf{p_c}$ denote the vector of the log of prices after the change. The equivalent income (EI) is equal to[1]:

$$EI = exp\left[\log(m) + \mathbf{p'w} - \mathbf{p'_c w} + 0.5 * \mathbf{p'Bp} - 0.5 * \mathbf{p'_c Bp_c}\right] \quad (A.42)$$

## B.1    NONLINEAR PRICE CHANGES AND WELL-BEING

For some goods, pricing is not homogeneous across quantities consumed, a case often referred to as non-linear pricing. The generic term non-linear pricing refers to any case in which the tariff is not strictly proportional to the quantity purchased. This applies to regulated and non-regulated prices for goods where, to different levels of consumption, correspond different levels of prices. This is typically the case of utilities such as electricity or water where the price is set according to the consumed quantity. For simplicity, assume that we have two goods, electricity, which we call good 1, and the rest of goods which we call good 2. Further, assume that the price of electricity is defined by two blocks of consumed quantities as follows (Table B.1):

Our aim is to derive the $EV$ and $CV$ welfare measurements in the case of non-linear pricing for the simple CD function. To introduce the proposed approach, first, consider the illustrative example in Table B.2.

Also, assume that the consumer maximizes its utility by spending 40$ and consumes 22 units. It is worth noting that proposing a simple functional form of consumer preferences with the presence of non-linear pricing schedule is not an easy task. However, we attempt to make this feasible based on the following proposition.

**Proposition 1 (Adequacy of Preferences Under the Veiled Schedule of Prices)** *The consumer behavior is independent of the exact non-linear structure of the price schedule, but it can be based on its equivalent average price schedule.*

---

[1] See also Hoareau and Tiberti (2014) for the definition of elasticities of the EASI model.

**Table B.1**   The price schedule

| Block | Price |
|---|---|
| 1 : 0 − q1 | $p_{1,1}$ |
| 2: $q_1$ and more | $p_{1,2}$ |

**Table B.2**   Nonlinear price schedule: an illustrative example

| Block | Price | Consumed quantity | Cost |
|---|---|---|---|
| 1:[0–10] | 1 | 10 | 10 |
| 2:[10–16] | 2 | 6 | 12 |
| 3:[16 and more] | 3 | 6 | 18 |
| Total | | 22 | 40 |

To better clarify this idea, assume that the seller will not indicate on the bill prices for each block of consumed quantities, but simply reveals the total amount for the total quantities consumed. A rational consumer should not be indifferent to how the bill is computed. However, this consumer must select the desired quantity based on its total cost in order to maximize its utility. The equivalent average price, for a given consumer, is simply the average price for the bought quantity. In the example above, the equivalent average price is equal to $40/22$. Remark that different schedule prices can generate the same cost or average price. Thus, it is also irrational to suppose that the marginal price is enough to model the consumer behavior. Given the constant expenditure shares assumed by the CD model, consider the following two cases:

A- The seller adopts a linear price structure and increases the single price from $40/22=1.81$ to $40/20.5=1.95$.

B- The seller adopts a non-linear price structure and increases the price in the third bracket from 3 to 4. With a fixed budget of 18, consumed quantities in the third bracket are reduced to 4.5.

Therefore, in both cases, the consumer can buy the same quantity of 20.5 with a budget of 40$. If the veil on price schedule exists, the optimal utility in each of the two cases will be the same. Note that with CD preferences, we have $\tau_{h,k} = p_{h,k}^b / p_{h,k}^a = q_{h,k}^a / q_{h,k}^b$, where $p_{h,k}$ refers to the average price (linear or non-linear cases). By assuming that initial prices are normalized to one, the equivalent variation can be redefined as follows:

$$EV_h = m_h \left( \frac{1}{\prod_1^K \tau_{h,k}{}^{\alpha_{h,k}}} - 1 \right) \tag{B.1}$$

$$CV_h = m_h \left( 1 - \prod_1^K \tau_{h,k}{}^{\alpha_{h,k}} \right) \tag{B.2}$$

Based on the level of expenditures on good $k$ and the new price schedule, we can easily estimate the component $\tau_{h,k}$. The lesson here is that the non-linearity of prices is not translated into different consumer preferences. It is the budget constraint that reduces the space of choices.

# C.1    STATA CODES

```
/************************* THE STATA CODE: A *****************************************/
/* Estimating the LV, PV,  EV, CV and CS welfare change measurements               */
/* Equations : LV->(3.3)|PV->(3.4)|EV->(3.13)|CV->(3.15)|CS-> (3.7)|CS_ELAS->(3.20)*/
/************************************************************************************/
/* ==============================================================================*/
/* Input information                                                             */
/* ==============================================================================*/
/* - List of varnames of per capita expenditures on the different goods          */
/* - List of price changes                                                       */
/* - To estimate the expenditures after the price change the assumption is        */
/*    that the preferences are homothetic                                         */
/* ==============================================================================*/
/* Outputs:  Change in welfare :LV, PV,  EV, PV, CS and CS_ELAS  variables         */
/************************************************************************************/
// Constructing the hypothetical data
clear
set obs  1000
set seed 1234
gen income    = uniform()*_n
gen food      = ( 0.3 + 0.2*uniform() )*income
gen clothes   = ( 0.1 + 0.1*uniform() )*income

// Initializing  the lists of items and price changes
local list_of_items   food clothes // list of items
local price_changes  0.06  0.04      // proportions of price changes
// Estimating the welfare change with LV and PV measurements
gen LV = 0       // Initializing the variable LV
gen PV = 0       // Initializing the variable PV
gen EV = 0       // Initializing the variable EV
gen CV = 0       // Initializing the variable CV
gen CS = 0       // Initializing the variable CS
gen CS_ELAS = 0 // Initializing the variable CS

local i = 1            // number  of the item.
foreach item of local list_of_items {
tempvar item_`i'
gen `item_`i'' = `item'
tempvar share_`i'
gen `share_`i'' = `item_`i''/income  // The expenditure shares
local nitems = `i'
local i = `i' + 1
}
local i = 1            // number  of the item.
foreach dp of local price_changes {
local dp_`i' = `dp'
local i = `i' + 1
}
tempvar price_index
gen  `price_index ' = 1    // Initializing the Laspeyres price index
forvalues i=1/`nitems' {
tempvar item_a
gen `item_a ' = `item_`i''            // The expenditures in period (a)
replace LV=LV - `dp_`i''*`item_a '
tempvar item_b
gen `item_b ' = (`item_a ')/(1+`dp_`i'') // The expenditures in period (b)
replace PV=PV - `dp_`i''*`item_b '
replace CS=CS - `item_a ' *ln(1+`dp_`i'')
replace CS_ELAS=CS_ELAS - `item_a '*`dp_`i''*(1 - 0.5*`dp_`i''*(1+`dp_`i''))
replace `price_index '=`price_index '*((1+`dp_`i'')^`share_`i'')
}
replace EV = income * ( 1/`price_index ' - 1 )
replace CV = income * ( 1 - `price_index '   )
/************************************************************************************/
```

```
/*********************** THE STATA CODE: B ****************************/
/* Estimating the  EV, PV and CS welfare change measurements         */
/* Approach : Taylor approximation                                   */
/* Order 1 :  CV=EV=CS = LV                                          */
/* Order 2 :  CV--> (3.52) || EV--> (3.53) || CS--> (3.54)          */
/*******************************************************************/
/* ==============================================================*/
/* Input information                                             */
/* ==============================================================*/
/* - List of varnames of per capita expenditures on the different goods */
/* - List of price changes                                       */
/* - The assumption :  the preferences are homothetic            */
/*******************************************************************/
/* ==============================================================*/
/* Outputs :  Change in welfare :  EV, CV and CS  variables      */
/*******************************************************************/
// Constructing the hypothetical data
clear
set obs  1000
set seed 1234
gen income     = uniform()*_n
gen food       = ( 0.3 + 0.2*uniform() )*income
gen clothes    = ( 0.1 + 0.1*uniform() )*income
// Initializing the lists of items and price changes
local list_of_items  food clothes // list of items
local price_changes  0.06 0.04    // proportions of price changes
// Setting the order of Taylor approximation
local order = 2 // The user can set the taylor order to 1.

// Estimating the welfare change with LV and PV measurements
gen LV                  = 0
gen EV_TAYLOR_'order'  = 0      // Initializing the variable EV
gen CV_TAYLOR_'order'  = 0      // Initializing the variable CV
gen CS_TAYLOR_'order'  = 0      // Initializing the variable CS
local i = 1                     // number  of the item.

foreach item of local list_of_items {
local item_'i' = " 'item'"
dis 'item_'i''
tempvar share_'i'
gen 'share_'i'' = 'item_'i''/income  // The expenditure shares
local nitems = 'i'
local i = 'i' + 1
}
local i = 1               // number  of the item.
foreach dp of local price_changes {
local dp_'i' = 'dp'
local i = 'i' + 1
}

forvalues i=1/'nitems' {
replace EV_TAYLOR_'order'=EV_TAYLOR_'order' - 'dp_'i''*'item_'i''
replace CV_TAYLOR_'order'=CV_TAYLOR_'order' - 'dp_'i''*'item_'i''
replace CS_TAYLOR_'order'=CS_TAYLOR_'order' - 'dp_'i''*'item_'i''

if 'order' >= 2 {
forvalues j=1/'nitems' {
replace EV_TAYLOR_'order' = EV_TAYLOR_'order' - 0.5 * (  -'share_'i''*'item_'j''  ///
-'item_'i''*('i'=='j'))*'dp_'i''*'dp_'j''
replace CV_TAYLOR_'order' = CV_TAYLOR_'order' - 0.5 * (  'share_'i''*'item_'j''  - ///
'item_'i''*('i'=='j'))*'dp_'i''*'dp_'j''
replace CS_TAYLOR_'order' = CS_TAYLOR_'order' - 0.5 * (0                        - ///
'item_'i''*('i'=='j'))*'dp_'i''*'dp_'j''
}
}
}
if 'order' >= 3 {
forvalues i=1/'nitems' {
forvalues j=1/'nitems' {
forvalues k=1/'nitems' {
replace EV_TAYLOR_'order' = EV_TAYLOR_'order' - ///
1/3* (('share_'i''* ('share_'j''*'item_'k'' +'item_'j'')*('i'=='j'=='k'))   + ///
('share_'i''*'item_'k''   + 'item_'i''))*('i'=='j'=='k') )*'dp_'i''*'dp_'j''*'dp_'k''

replace CV_TAYLOR_'order' = CV_TAYLOR_'order' - ///
1/3* (( -'share_'i''* ('share_'j''*'item_'k''+ 'item_'j'')*('i'=='j'=='k')) + ///
( - 'share_'i''*'item_'k''   + 'item_'i''))*('i'=='j'=='k') )*'dp_'i''*'dp_'j''*'dp_'k''
```

```
replace CS_TAYLOR_'order' = CS_TAYLOR_'order' - ///
  1/3  * (    'item_'i''*('i'=='j'=='k'))*'dp_'i''*'dp_'j''*'dp_'k''
  }
 }
 }
 }
/***************************************************************************/


/*********************** THE STATA CODE: C *******************************/
/* - The Vartia(1983) algorithm                                         */
/* - Approach: Numerical approximation                                  */
/* - Outputs:  Change in welfare :        CV-> (3.64)  //  EV-> (3.65)  */
/* - The user can increase the number of goods or use another demand    */
/*    function                                                          */
/***************************************************************************/

set trace off
mata: mata clear
mata
num=10                          /* Number of partitions or iterations */

//Initializing the parameters (prices and income)
real matrix function initialise_parameters(scalar t)
{
if (t==0) return (1.0   \ 1.0 \ 1.0 )  /* Initial price vector */
if (t==1) return (1.3   \ 1.4 \ 1.7 )  /* Final   price vector */
if (t==2) return (0.3   \ 0.5 \ 0.2 )  /* income shares        */
if (t==3) return (100)                 /* Income               */
}

// Defining the demand function
real matrix function eval_quantities(real matrix x)
{
real matrix q
alpha  =initialise_parameters(2)
n=cols(x)-1
n1=n+1
q = J(1,n,0)
for (r=1; r<=n; r++) {
q[r]=alpha[r]:*x[n1]:/x[r]  // Evaluate quantities
}
return(q)
}

p0        =    initialise_parameters(0)
p1        =    initialise_parameters(1)
alpha     =    initialise_parameters(2)
y_cv_old  =    initialise_parameters(3)
y_ev_old  =    initialise_parameters(3)
y0        =    initialise_parameters(3)

y_cv=y0
y_ev=y0
tcv = 0
tev = 0
cv=0
ev=0

del  = (p1:-p0)/num
dp=p1:-p0
par   = J(rows(alpha)+1,1,.)
par[1..rows(alpha)]=p0
par[rows(alpha)+1]=y0
q_cv_old=eval_quantities(par')

par[1..rows(alpha)]=p1
par[rows(alpha)+1]=y0
q_ev_old=eval_quantities(par')

for (i=1; i<=num; ++i) {
// initializing parameters for local derivatives (CV)
a_cv  = J(rows(alpha),1,1)
a_cv  = (((a_cv:*(i-1)):/num):*dp):+1  // prices at step i for CV
par_cv  = J(rows(alpha)+1,1,.)
par_cv[1..rows(alpha)]=a_cv
```

```
par_cv[rows(alpha)+1]=y_cv
q_cv_new = eval_quantities(par_cv')

// initializing parameters for local derivatives (EV)
a_ev   = J(rows(alpha),1,1)
a_ev   = -(((a_ev:*(i-1))::/num):*dp):+p1 // prices at step i for EV
par_ev  = J(rows(alpha)+1,1,.)
par_ev[1..rows(alpha)]=a_ev
par_ev[rows(alpha)+1]=y_ev
q_ev_new = eval_quantities(par_ev')

cv =   (0.5*(q_cv_old:+q_cv_new))*del
ev =   (0.5*(q_cv_old:+q_cv_new))*del

y_cv = y_cv+cv
y_ev = y_ev-ev

tcv = tcv-cv
tev = tev-ev

q_cv_old = q_cv_new
q_ev_old = q_cv_new
}

tcv
tev

end

clear all
local price_index =((1.3)^0.3)*((1.4)^0.5)*((1.7)^0.2)
dis 'True CV = ' 100 * (1- 'price_index' )
dis 'True EV = ' 100 * (1/'price_index' -1)


/************************** THE STATA CODE: D ***************************/
/* - The Breslaw and Barry's (1995) algorithm                         */
/* - Approach: Numerical approximation                                */
/* - Outputs:  Change in welfare: EV, CV-> (3.66)                     */
/* - The algorithm is programmed with Stata (exactly with mata). mata is */
/*   the matrix language of Stat                                      */
/* - The user can increase the number of goods or use another demand  */
/*   function                                                         */
/**********************************************************************/

set more off
mata: mata clear
mata
num=10                              /* Number of iterations */
real matrix function initialise_parameters(scalar t)
{
if (t==0) return (1.0   \ 1.0 \ 1.0 )  /* Initial price vector */
if (t==1) return (1.3   \ 1.4 \ 1.7 )  /* Final   price vector */
if (t==2) return (0.3   \ 0.5 \ 0.2 )  /* income shares        */
if (t==3) return (100)                 /* Income               */
}

// Defining the Marshallian demand functions
// Parameters: x_1...x_n (prices) and x_{n+1} income
real matrix function eval_quantities(real matrix x)
{
real matrix q
alpha =initialise_parameters(2)
n=cols(x)-1
n1=n+1
q = J(1,n,0)
for (r=1; r<=n; r++) {
q[r]=alpha[r]:*x[n1]:/x[r]  // Evaluate quantities
}
return(q)
}

void eval_t2(x, v) // function used for the numerical derivative
{
alpha =initialise_parameters(2)
n=cols(x)-1
n1=n+1
```

```
v = J(1,n1,.)
v[1..n]=eval_quantities(x)   // Evaluate the quantities
v[n1] = x[n1]                // Evaluate the income
}

D = deriv_init()  // function used for the num. derivative

p0      =   initialise_parameters(0)
p1      =   initialise_parameters(1)
alpha   =   initialise_parameters(2)
y_cv    =   initialise_parameters(3)
y_ev    =   initialise_parameters(3)
tcv = 0
tev = 0
del  = (p1:-p0)/num
ndel = -del
dp=p1:-p0
for (i=1; i<=num; ++i) {

a_cv    = J(rows(alpha),1,1)
a_cv    = (((a_cv:*(i-1)):/num):*dp):+1 // prices at step i for CV

a_ev    = J(rows(alpha),1,1)
a_ev    = -(((a_ev:*(i-1)):/num):*dp):+p1 // prices at step i for EV

// initializing parameters for local derivatives (CV)
par_cv    = J(rows(alpha)+1,1,.)
par_cv[1..rows(alpha)]=a_cv
par_cv[rows(alpha)+1]=y_cv
par_cv
// initializing parameters for local derivatives (EV)
par_ev    = J(rows(alpha)+1,1,.)
par_ev[1..rows(alpha)]=a_ev
par_ev[rows(alpha)+1]=y_ev

h_cv=eval_quantities(par_cv')    // quantities at step i for CV
h_ev=eval_quantities(par_ev')    // quantities at step i for EV

deriv_init_evaluator(D, &eval_t2())
deriv_init_evaluatortype(D, "t")

deriv_init_params(D, par_cv')
AA=deriv(D, 1)[1::rows(alpha),1..rows(alpha)+1]
A1 = AA[1::rows(alpha),1..rows(alpha)] // derivative with respect to prices
A2 = AA[1::rows(alpha),rows(alpha)+1] // derivative with respect to income
dhdp_cv = A1+A2*h_cv'

deriv_init_params(D, par_ev')
AA=deriv(D, 1)[1::rows(alpha),1..rows(alpha)+1]
A1=AA[1::rows(alpha),1..rows(alpha)]  // derivative with respect to prices
A2 = AA[1::rows(alpha),rows(alpha)+1] // derivative with respect to income
dhdp_ev = A1+A2*h_ev'
// See the equation (68)
cv =  del'*h_cv + 0.5*del'*dhdp_cv*del
ev =  ndel'*h_ev + 0.5*ndel'*dhdp_ev*ndel

tcv=tcv-cv
tev=tev+ev

y_cv=y_cv+cv
y_ev=y_ev+ev

}
tcv
tev
end

clear all
local price_index=((1.3)^0.3)*((1.4)^0.5)*((1.7)^0.2)
dis "True CV = " 100 * (1- 'price_index' )
dis "True EV = " 100 * (1/'price_index' -1)


/********************** THE STATA CODE: E ***************************/
/* - The Euler and RK4 algorithms                                  */
/* - Approach: Numerical approximation                             */
/* - Outputs:  Change in welfare: EV/CV->  (3.67) and (3.68)       */
```

```
'
/* — The user can increase the number of goods or use another demand      */
/*   function                                                             */
/***************************************************************************/
local m       = 100       // Income
local niter   = 12        // Number of iterations
// By default , we estimate the EV. The user can set this to be "CV".
local measurement = "EV"

// expenditures shares (alpha's values). The user can change the number of items
matrix alpha = (0.10 \ 0.05 \ 0.12 \ 0.06)

matrix p0    = (1.00 \ 1.00 \ 1.00 \ 1.00 ) // Initial prices
matrix p1    = (1.15 \ 1.30 \ 1.10 \ 1.25)  // Final prices

local price_index =1
local nitems = rowsof(alpha)        // Number of items
// loading the different values in local macros.
forvalues k=1/'nitems ' {
local alpha_ 'k' = el(alpha, 'k',1)
local p'k'_0 = el(p0, 'k',1)
local p'k'_1 = el(p1, 'k',1)
local price_index='price_index '*( 'p'k'_1'^'alpha_ 'k'')

if " 'measurement'"=="CV"  {
local h'k'  = ('p'k'_1—'p'k'_0)/'niter '
local multi = (1/'price_index ' —1)
}

if " 'measurement'"=="EV"  {
local multi = (1 — 'price_index ')
local h'k'  = —('p'k'_1'—'p'k'_0')/'niter '
forvalues k=1/'nitems ' {
local alpha_ 'k' = el(alpha, 'k',1)
local p'k'_1 = el(p0, 'k',1)
local p'k'_0 = el(p1, 'k',1)
}
}
}
local m0     = 100
local me0    = 100

// A simple program to evaluate the first derivative : the case of Cobb–Douglas function.
cap program drop odf
program define odf, rclass
args p m alpha
 return scalar ft = —'alpha '*'m'/('p')
end

// The iterative algorithm for the Euler and RK4 methods.
forvalues i=1/'niter ' {
local j='i'—1

forvalues k=1/'nitems ' {
local p_'k'_0 ='p'k'_0'
local m_'k'   = 'm'j''
local mm_'k'  = 'm'j''
local p_'k'_'i '    = 'p_'k'_0'+'h'k''*'i '
local p_'k'         = 'p_'k'_'j''
odf 'p_'k''  'm_'k''  'alpha_ 'k''

local k1_'k' = 'r(ft )'
local p_'k' = 'p_'k'_'j''+0.5*'h'k''
local m_'k'='mm_'k''+0.5*'k1_'k''*'h'k''
odf 'p_'k''  'm_'k''  'alpha_ 'k''
local k2_'k' = 'r(ft )'
local m_'k'='mm_'k''+0.5*'k2_'k''*'h'k''
odf 'p_'k''  'm_'k''  'alpha_ 'k''
local k3_'k' = 'r(ft )'

local p_'k'  = 'p_'k'_'i''
local m_'k'='mm_'k''+'k3_'k''*'h'k''
odf 'p_'k''  'm_'k''  'alpha_ 'k''
local k4_'k' = 'r(ft )'

local c'i' = 'c'i''+1/6*('k1_'k''+2*('k2_'k''+'k3_'k''))+'k4_'k'')*'h'k''
local ce'i'= 'ce'i''+ 1*('k4_'k'')*'h'k''
}
```

```
local m'i'  =  'm'j'' + 'c'i''
local me'i'  =  'me'j''+ 'ce'i''
if ''measurement''=='CV' di "Iteration ''i'      ": 'measurement'_Euler: '  ///
  'me'i'' - 'me0'  '| 'measurement'_RK4: '     'm'i'' - 'm0'
if ''measurement''=='EV' di "Iteration ''i'      ": 'measurement'_Euler: '  ///
  - 'me'i'' + 'me0'  '| 'measurement'_RK4: ' - 'm'i'' + 'm0'
}
```

```
// The true value of the EV/CV measurement
dis 'True value of 'measurement' = ' 100 * 'multi'
```

# REFERENCES

BANKS, J., R. BLUNDELL, AND A. LEWBEL (1997): "Quadratic Engel Curves And Consumer Demand," *The Review of Economics and Statistics*, 79, 527–539.

DEATON, A. AND J. MUELLBAUER (1980): "An Almost Ideal Demand System," *American Economic Review*, 70, 312–336.

HOAREAU S., LACROIX G., H. M. AND L. TIBERTI (2014): "Exact Affine Stone Index Demand System in R: The easi Package," Tech. rep., University Laval, CIRPEE: https://cran.r-project.org/web/packages/easi/index.html.

LEWBEL, A. AND K. PENDAKUR (2009): "Tricks with Hicks: The EASI Demand System," *American Economic Review*, 99, 827–63.

# INDEX

**B**
Breslaw and Smith approximation, 40

**C**
Cobb–Douglas (CD) function, 25, 36–37, 60, 77
Compensating variation, 2, 11–16, 19, 22, 23, 25–27, 32–34, 36–40, 42–44, 48, 50, 56, 60, 75, 76, 87, 89
Consumer surplus, 3, 11

**D**
Demand functions
  almost Ideal Demand System (AIDS), 4, 53, 82–84
  exact Affine Stone Index (EASI), 4, 53, 85–87
  Hicksian, 10, 31
  Linear Demand, 79
  linear Expenditure System (LES), 4, 53, 80–82
  log Linear demand, 79
  Marshallian, 4, 10, 11, 14, 37, 39, 42, 58
  quadratic Almost Ideal System (QUAIDS), 4, 53, 84–85
Differential equations, 38

**E**
Elasticity
  income elasticity, 44, 81, 85
  non compensated price elasticity, 51, 85
Equivalent variation (EV), 2, 5, 11, 12, 81, 89
Euler method, 41, 42

**I**
Income effect, 3, 26, 31, 32, 34, 50, 76
Index numbers, 13, 19, 20
Individual welfare, 6, 48, 61, 67

© The Author(s) 2019
A. Araar, P. Verme, *Prices and Welfare*,
https://doi.org/10.1007/978-3-030-17423-1

**L**
Laspeyres
  index, 5, 13, 20, 32
  variation, 2, 11, 13

**P**
Paasche
  index, 5, 13
  variation, 2, 11, 13
Pro-poor curves, 64, 69–73

**R**
Runge and Kutta method, 41

**S**
Social welfare, 10, 48, 61, 64, 67
Stata codes, 90–96
Statistical inference, 6, 64–69

Stochastic dominance, 64, 69–73
Substitution effect, 3, 19, 26–28,
    30–32, 34–36, 41, 47, 50, 51,
    54, 61, 75

**T**
Taylor's approximations
  first order, 31, 76
  higher orders, 3, 76

**U**
Utility
  direct, 31
  indirect, 10, 13, 38, 58, 81, 84, 85

**V**
Vartia's approximation, 38–40